CRITICISM AND CREATION

CRITICISM AND CREATION

ESSAYS AND ADDRESSES

By

Herbert J. C. Grierson

*Emeritus Professor of Rhetoric & English Literature
in the University of Edinburgh*

1949

CHATTO AND WINDUS

LONDON

PUBLISHED BY
Chatto & Windus
LONDON

*

Clarke, Irwin & Co. Ltd
TORONTO

PRINTED IN GREAT BRITAIN BY
J. W. ARROWSMITH LTD., BRISTOL

Prefatory Note

THE essays in this volume have all been issued separately. The three which follow the Deneke Lecture appeared in the *Modern Language Review* as articles or reviews. That on *Verse Translation* was my address as President of the English Association in 1948. It was printed in *Essays and Studies by Members of the English Association* collected by Nora Ellis-Fermor in 1944.

Contents

Criticism and Creation: Their Interactions

Criticism and Creation: Their Interactions

Being the Deneke Lecture, Lady Margaret Hall, Oxford,
14 February, 1941, with some modifications.

WHAT is the relation of the critic to the work of the
creative artist ? What is he trying to do when he
comments on a play by Shakespeare or a poem by Wordsworth ? The general answer to-day would be that he is
the interpreter to less appreciative readers, a valuator
indicating what the poet has set himself to do; how far he
has succeeded or fallen short, and what is the final worth
of the work, if the author has succeeded in his aim or, it
may be, achieved something else by the way. 'It is a very
good office,' says Hazlitt, 'one man does another when he
tells him the manner of his being pleased'. But the critic
has not always been content with such a limited view of
his function. He has often, very definitely at certain periods,
and still at times, been tempted to think that he may be an
instructor not only to other readers but to the poet, that his
judgments are based on principles, irrefragable principles,
the neglect of which it is his duty to point out, judged by
which principles it became a duty to condemn, for example,
the *Cid* of Corneille notwithstanding the approval which it
had gained from the distinguished audiences that crowded
Mondory's theatre. Such a condemnation might, of course,
represent the reaction of a more understanding and culti-
vated taste correcting the too facile response of a mixed
audience to a somewhat cheap appeal. But that was not
the claim made by the Academy when it acted at the
instance of Richelieu. It was that they were the defenders
of certain laws which Corneille had violated, laws of the
drama as definite and authoritative in their sphere as the

laws which govern our conduct or the, perhaps still more rigid, laws of social etiquette. And this was the claim of Renaissance criticism as it took its rise in Italy and pervaded the critical writings of Western Europe. It spoke as a lawgiver, though it is worth noting at the outset of what I have to discuss that in just those countries where the creative spirit was strongest, notably in the drama in Spain and England, this authoritative criticism had least practical effect, even when it received a polite acquiescence in any critical discussion.

The source of this authoritative criticism was, I fear, the *Poetics* of Aristotle rightly or wrongly understood. Is the *Poetics* a valuable, though too fragmentary, treatise on aesthetics, or as I think the late Professor A. E. Taylor declared, a practical handbook for the composition of melodramas ? It is not for me to say. It contains three interesting words, *mimesis, catharsis, hamartia*, about the exact import of which the critics are still much divided. Our admiration of the philosophic, scientific theorizing of the Greeks has a little obscured our perception of their strongly practical bent. Bacon was not, as Macaulay thought, the first philosopher who theorized with a view to action, to conduct. Plato did not regard himself as a speculative dreamer in the sphere of morals and politics. It was his ambition to influence, to guide rulers who would lend an ear. I doubt if Aristotle regarded his *Ethics* as purely speculative. At any rate the *Poetics* was composed in close connexion with the most practical, and the most complete in the achievement of its end, among all his treatises. In the *Rhetoric*, it has been said with justice, the art of persuasion, as based on a thorough knowledge of human nature, was set forth so fully that nothing of importance has ever been added. When indeed with the disappearance of liberty eloquence grew, as Milton says, ' mute '—it is only in a free country that political discussion is permitted—then rhetoric became what the late Professor Saintsbury would

4

apparently have wished it to be, a study of the refinements and elaborations of prose style. For Saintsbury in the *History of Criticism* looks at the *Rhetoric* from an angle which disguises its real purpose. He seems to think, or speaks as if, Aristotle had intended to compose a *Prosaics* corresponding to the *Poetics*, but had been diverted and limited by the unfortunate preoccupation of the Greeks with the spoken word, with oratory. This is to put the cart before the horse. Aristotle had no thought of a *Prosaics*. His definition of Rhetoric was ' a faculty of discovering all the means of persuasion in any subject '. But the various means of persuasion, intellectual, moral, emotional, which he analyses and illustrates, are just as applicable in poetry as in prose, are made use of by the dramatists, as he points out in the *Poetics*, for you will remember that when he comes there to speak of *dianoia*, thought, he refers us at once to the *Rhetoric* : ' Under thought is included every effect which has to be produced by speech: in particular proof and refutation, the exciting of the feelings such as pity, fear, anger and the like.' Indeed there is hardly anything he says in the masterly second book of the *Rhetoric* about the exciting and allaying of feeling which may not be illustrated from the drama, Greek and Shakespearian.

Now the practical spirit which inspired the *Rhetoric* seems to me to have been that in which was composed or outlined what we know as the *Poetics*. Having analysed, with all the long experience behind him of argument, in oratory and discussion and drama in the Greek world, the factors which make for persuasion in matters about which scientific truth is unattainable, he would now, with the work of Homer and the tragedians in view, consider what are the factors which go to make a good poem, a good tragedy. Only the part concerning tragedy has survived and that probably only in part. But what he does thus elicit from a study of Sophocles, Euripides, and Homer is presented as rules, at least as hints for those who would be epic or tragic poets, especially the latter. 'A well-constructed plot *should* be single in its issue rather than double as some maintain.' 'They are in error who censure Euripides just because he follows this principle in his plays, many of which end unhappily. *It is*, as we have said, *the right ending.*' 'In respect of character there are four things to be aimed at. First and most important it *must be good*. Even a woman may be good and also a slave, though the woman may be said to be an inferior being and the slave quite worthless.' Much of what Aristotle said has stood the test of time and an extended experience, a knowledge of other forms of drama. Moreover many of his statements were only of a tentative kind. 'Tragedy *endeavours* as far as possible to confine itself to a single revolution of the sun, or but slightly to exceed this limit.'

It was the error of his followers, especially the Italian critics of the Renaissance, which converted Aristotle's suggestions, based on Greek Drama, into hard and fast rules any violation of which was in itself an aesthetic fault or crime. The general principles of that criticism have been well summarized by Saintsbury in the second volume of the *History of Criticism*—poetry as an imitation of Nature, the fixed kinds each with its own rules, those of tragedy well described by Aristotle, to whose rules must be added the Unities of Place and Time, the theory of the epic or heroic poem; and finally the all-embracing rule 'imitate the ancients'. Pope has condensed them in his *Essay on Criticism*:

> First follow Nature, and your judgement frame
> By her just standard, which is still the same:
> Unerring Nature, still divinely bright,
> One clear, unchang'd, and universal light,
> Life, force, and beauty, must to all impart,
> At once the source, and end, and test of Art.

But the critics have discovered the rules to be obeyed by whoever would follow Nature:

> Those rules of old discovered, not devised,
> Are Nature still, but Nature methodised;
> Nature, like Liberty, is but restrained
> By the same laws which first herself ordained.

And the Ancients are our great exemplars of poets who understood and followed Nature:

> When first young Maro in his boundless mind
> A work to outlast immortal Rome designed,
> Perhaps he seemed above the critics' law,
> And but from Nature's fountains scorned to draw:
> But when to examine every part he came,
> Nature and Homer were, he found, the same.
> Convinced, amazed, he checks the bold design:
> And rules as strict his laboured work confine,
> As if the Stagirite o'erlooked each line.
> Learn hence for ancient rules a just esteem;
> To copy Nature is to copy them.

I have no intention of elaborating or discussing this criticism as such. What I wish to do is something different. It is to consider how the rules worked, what influence for good or evil they effected, when they were accepted more or less in their entirety by poets of genius, creative poets or dramatists. If my time allows, I may endeavour to consider occasional later suggestions that the critic may undertake to prescribe for the artist.

The first sharp collision of this law-giving criticism with poetry of undeniable merit and achieved popularity occurred in Italy over the *Orlando Furioso* of Ariosto. Here was a poem which every reader enjoyed but lo! and behold! it violated all the rules of Heroic poetry. The subject was not historical, and it lacked unity of plot. What was one to think ? Trissino undertook to show what a Heroic poem

should be like and composed an *Italia Liberata*, which may
obey the rules but unfortunately is unreadable. Giraldi took
up the defence of the *Romanzi* on the good ground which
unfortunately the critics would not adhere to, viz., that
' the romance is a poetic kind of which Aristotle did not
know, and to which his rules do not apply. Italian literature
need not follow the rules of Greek poetry.' But the blessed
doctrine of the kinds had to be respected and new rules
elaborated for this new kind. The final result of the controversy was the *Gerusalemme Liberata* of Tasso whose endeavour was to combine the charms of romance, i.e. love and
magic, with the historical theme and unity of the epic,
the classical epic. Much ink was spilled over the relative
merits of Ariosto and Tasso, but what survives is just their
poems, and you are free to enjoy either or both. Both
had a shaping influence on Spenser, for he too knew about
the rules, as Professor Renwick has demonstrated, but the
rules have nothing to do with the interest of his *Faerie
Queene*.

But it was about the drama that critical controversy
chiefly centred and it was on the stage that observance of
the rules could be enforced or experimented with; and
what I wish to study briefly is their effect on the drama,
confining myself mainly to tragedy, to the tragedies of
the *dioscuri* of the French stage, Corneille and Racine, to
compare what happened in France with the attempt in
our more individualistic country to ' correct ' English drama
and poetry, an attempt made single-handed on the Elizabethan stage by ' rare Ben Jonson ' and later in epic and
drama by a greater than Jonson, John Milton. The history
of the evolution of French tragedy is very interesting.
French men of letters have always been more concerned
about the theory of their art than our poets or dramatists
or artists generally are. They love a ' definite banner and
a clear programme '. Indeed Renaissance, which ultimately
became Classical, French poetry and drama opened with

8

a programme, the *Défense et Illustration de la Langue Française* of du Bellay, in which French poets are enjoined to discard the confectionery (épicerie) of medieval poetry and create for France a new poetry in the natural forms, discovered and sanctioned by the Ancients—Epic, Ode, Satire, Epigram, Pastoral, and Drama, tragedy and comedy distinguished not blended. To these was added one form, not classical in origin but Italian, and perfected by Petrarch, the sonnet. This became the programme of the Pleiad whose chief poet was Ronsard and dramatist Robert Garnier. Garnier's Senecan, declamatory, and lyrical tragedies had a considerable effect without as well as within France. There is an echo of a phrase of Garnier in *Hamlet*, which lends some small support to the view that Kyd had a hand in the original *Hamlet*, for Kyd translated the *Cornélie* of Garnier. But the fault of all these Senecan tragedies, as of our own *Gorboduc* and *Misfortunes of Arthur*, is that they have no dramatic life, no interest of plot developed through character.

Classical French tragedy as it finally took shape in the plays of Corneille and Racine had a complex origin, three different roots. First there is the demand of the audience for a play which interests them by the appeal of story and suspense, which in the drama, as Hardy, the ancestor of later drama, found when he came to Paris, was represented by story plays not unlike our own but influenced by the Spanish tragi-comedy with its heightened element of suspense and surprise. In its final development the French was to be an extreme representative of a drama in which, even more than in the Greek, every scene, every soliloquy, every line was a step in the psychological development of the surprising catastrophe. The second was this literary theory, the rules, supported, as the critics believed, by the example of the tragedies of Seneca and, behind these, of Greek tragedy. What the rules required were (1) an historical base for tragedy, not an invented, romantic story;

(2) propriety, what Voltaire calls 'bienséance'— the hero must be heroic, a soldier always soldierly, no one of lower rank may strike one above him, &c; and (3) a rigid adherence to the Unities of Place and Time. To Voltaire these last are the 'fundamental rules of the theatre . . . it implies feebleness and sterility to extend an action beyond the proper space of time and place of action'. According to the same authority they are more essential than the rule of propriety, decorum, which Milton pronounces to be 'the grand master to observe'. As a fact the rules derive partly from Aristotle, partly from a mistake taken over from Castelvetro regarding the nature of dramatic representation, which Dr. Johnson was the first to expose when he pointed out that no one in his right mind believed the actors on the stage to be real characters in a real action. They are playing a part, and there is no more reason that one should not go off the stage in London and reappear on the other side in Rome or Pekin than that one chapter of a story should end in one place and the next begin in another. There may of course be another, an aesthetic justification of the Unities, and that comes into consideration when I pass to my third factor, the emergence of writers of real dramatic power.

Hardy was a great admirer of the poetry of the Pleiad but his own efforts at style were not happy. Nor did he himself attach importance to the Unities. He tightened up the story, but with little or no real dramatic interest. For a dramatic poet or dramatic novelist the interest of plot, of suspense, will depend, not on what happens, the *Deus ex Machina*, whatever shape that may take from the intervention of a God or King to the death of a wealthy uncle. The interest for him is what certain people are and feel and think and do. Critics have spoken of Christopher Marlowe as though the sole merit of *Tamburlaine* was the new grandeur, or bombast, of style and the verse. That is not the whole truth, nor the most important truth, which is that in *Tamburlaine*, however crudely, the centre of interest is found neither in the 'sentences' of the Senecan drama nor the crude happenings of the popular plays, e.g. *Cambyses* or *Sir Clyomon and Sir Clamydas*, but in the soul of a man 'like his desire lift upward and divine'. Just so was it with the first great French tragedy, *Le Cid* of Corneille. When in that play Rodrigue, the Cid, who has killed the father of Chimène to whom he is betrothed, killed him in defence of his own father's honour, meets her on the stage, 'a shudder', it was said, 'ran through the audience assembled in Mondory's theatre indicating a marvellous curiosity, a redoubling of attention as to what they could have to say to one another in so pitiable a situation'. That is the dramatic interest proper. In the final solution the war and the King do play somewhat the part of an intervening providence. But it is on such problems of conduct, resolutions in a crisis, that the interest of Corneille's tragedies depends, notably in *Cinna*, a play of the interaction of character of singular nobility. The dialogue in a French tragedy never is, as not infrequently in Shakespeare, a poetic digression, at least a pause in the main action, talk about the drinking customs of the Danes, &c. All is there to promote the conflict of motives from which the catastrophe issues.

The success of the *Cid* evoked a storm of jealous criticism among Corneille's fellow dramatists. Scudéry appealed to the recently founded Academy, and Chapelain drew up a report almost at the dictation of Richelieu, himself a disappointed dramatist, in which the *Cid* was condemned as wanting in that art which Jonson found Shakespeare defective in, and which Milton calls 'that sublime art which in Aristotle's *Poetics*, in Horace and the Italian commentaries of Castelvetro, Tasso, Mazzini and others teaches what the laws are of a true epic poem, what of a dramatic, what of a lyric, what decorum is which is the grand master to observe'.

Thus in its final form French tragedy was the outcome of a conflict between the creative genius of Corneille and Racine and the so-called rules enforced by a pedantic but in France powerful authority. It was not, however, the observance of the rules which justified the two dramatists. It was they who justified, so far as that could be done, the rules, by developing a type of tragedy to which the observance, or an approximation to the observance, of them was used to lend a heightened interest, raise the mood of suspense to its intensest level, and that is a drama in which everything is subordinated to the relentless, dramatic logic by which a single critical action is worked out to a surprising solution, the surprise depending in Corneille's plays on a sudden elevation of moral feeling, an *élan*; in Racine on the subtle evolution of feeling, the eddying, flowing, and sudden turns of feeling in a woman's heart. ' Qui te l'a dit ? '

Let me take one example of a tragedy in which a critical action is developed naturally and easily in the space of a day or less. But before doing so I will recall a Greek tragedy which Aristotle seems to have thought the best example of a tragic plot, the *Oedipus Tyrannus*, the action of which is also comprehended within the compass of a day. I have said that a dramatic plot is one in which the interest centres, not in what happens, but in what the characters feel and think and in consequence do. Now there is character in the *Oedipus*, the hot temper of Oedipus, the slow anger of Teiresias, the hard virtue of Creon, the passionate Jocasta. But the action of the play is mainly determined by what *happens*—the plague, the oracle, the almost accidental revelation of what has happened in the past. But what happens in a Greek tragedy is distinguished from the mere accident of tragi-comedy by the fact that it is the work of the Gods. They are always a factor in Greek tragedy— Apollo, the Furies, Artemis, Heracles, &c. There is nothing of the kind in French tragedy except the background,

grasped by faith, felt not seen, in Racine's two later tragedies, *Athalie* and *Esther*.   But returning to the question
of time, the play I wish to look at is the *Bérénice* of Racine.
Berenice, Queen of Palestine, has been living in Rome
loving and loved by Titus.   Thither has come an earlier
lover, Antiochus, King of Comagena.   Vespasian the
Emperor has died and Berenice is confident, and the Court
shares her confidence, that now set free Titus will marry
her despite the jealousy with which such a marriage is
regarded by the Romans:

> Rome hait tous les rois, et Bérénice est reine.

Nevertheless she is confident:

> Titus m'aime, il peut tout, il n'a plus qu'à parler.

Meantime Titus has gone into retreat for eight days.   It
is not till the second scene of the second act that we hear
him in conference with his confidant Paulin, consulting
him as to the sentiment of the Roman people.   He is told
what her own confidante has already whispered to Berenice:

> Elle a mille vertus, mais, seigneur, elle est reine.

The feeling of the people is inexorable: ' So do the Romans
regard your love, and I cannot answer but that the senate,
charged with the prayers of the whole empire, will repeat
here what I have just said, and that Rome falling on her
knees will demand a choice worthy of her and of you.'
But Titus has already made up his mind: ' Despite my
passion, Paulin, despite her charms, now that I could set
the crown on so many attractions, now that I love her
more than ever, when a happy marriage might pay in one
day for the desires of five years, I am going, Paulin, O
heavens, how can I say it ? '
  ' What, my Lord ? '
  ' To leave her for ever. Berenice has for long outweighed
victory, and if at last I lean to the side of glory, believe me,

O believe me, it has cost me, to conquer such a love, combats from which my heart will bleed for many a day. . . . The moment that heaven had recalled my father, that my hand had closed his eyes, I was disabused of my fond dream. I felt the burden imposed upon me. . . . What a disgrace for me if my first step had been to overthrow all the rights of Rome, to found my happiness on the ruin of her laws.' The conflict of feelings follows in Titus, in Berenice, in Antiochus portrayed as Racine loved to elaborate it, and ever moving forward to the catastrophe. But even when Titus learns from a letter he has snatched from her hand that it is Berenice's intention to kill herself, and his reply is that if she does so he will follow, even then he does not weaken in his resolve: ' Do not dream that wearied with so many fears I will dry your eyes by a happy marriage. To whatever extremity you have reduced me my glory pursues me inexorably. Unceasingly it presents to my astonished mind the empire as incompatible with my marriage to you, tells me that after the fame I have achieved less than ever ought I to marry you. Yes, Madam, and still less ought I to say to you that I am ready for your sake to abandon the empire, to follow you and, content with fetters, to sigh with you at the other end of the world. You yourself would blush for my cowardly conduct, would grieve to see marching in your suite an unworthy emperor deprived alike of empire and court.' Antiochus is ready also to make the decisive step, but standing between the two Berenice rises to the situation and dismissing the royal suitor, Antiochus, herself abandons Rome for ever. Line by line the tragedy has led you on expectant and wondering what the lovers will do, what, to recall the *Cid*, they will find to say in so pitiable a situation. There are no digressions, no speeches which delight us simply by their poetry, like the description of Ophelia's death, and no humours. I mean that we see Racine's characters only in relation to the single action. There are no such suggestions of manners and humours as we get even in the tragedies of Shakespeare, Hamlet's absent-mindedness and melancholy and careless dress of which we have almost a better knowledge than of the reasons for his delay, Macbeth's hallucinations, Othello's nobility of speech and carriage, &c.

The French did then develop a quite special type of tragedy which justified, even required, an acceptance of the Unity of time or a close approximation. The Unity of place was more of a stumbling-block, as Corneille distinctly stated, and of less importance: French tragedy is *not* Greek, and it is *not* Elizabethan.

For to pass to England is to pass from a people that loves logical theory, programmes, rules, to a people amongst whom the individual dominates. Speaking of the recent ' imagist ' movement in France an American critic writes: ' The medley of images; the deliberately mixed metaphors; the combination of passion and wit; the bold amalgamation of material with spiritual—all these may seem to the Englishman quite proper and familiar. He has always known them in the English poetry of the sixteenth and seventeenth centuries—Shakespeare and the other Elizabethans did all these things without theorizing about them. Is this not the natural language of poetry ? Is it not the norm against which the eighteenth-century diction was a heresy and to which the Romantics did their best to return ? ' Verlaine's claim, again, for music as the predominant in lyric was just Blake's and Shelley's. But to return to the sixteenth century, the rules found their way to England as to other countries, notably in Sidney's *Defence of Poesy*, where they are used to measure the defects of English drama in its early stages: ' Our tragedies and comedies not without cause cried out against, observing rules neither of honest civilities nor of skilful Poetry, Excepting *Gorboduc*—which notwithstanding as it is full of stately speeches and well-sounding phrases, climbing to the height of Seneca his style, and as full of notable morality which it doth most delightfully teach, and so obtain the very end of poetry, yet in truth it is very defective in two circumstances. . . . For it is faulty both in Place and Time, the two necessary companions of all corporal actions.' Sidney's admonitions had no effect on the evolution of the Elizabethan drama. That was directed by Marlowe, Greene, Peele, Lyly, Kyd, Shakespeare, and their work was to give dramatic interest and poetic beauty to the story play with a main plot but variety of incident and at times a subordinate plot. The form of a Shakespearian tragedy was determined by no critical rules enforced from without but shaped by what seemed to Shakespeare the nature and requirements of the story itself—the rush, pause, and final rush of *Macbeth*, the slow opening and gathering speed of *Othello*, the succession of impressive scenes with no real forward movement of *Hamlet*, the rapid shifting stormy scenes of *Lear*. Shakespeare knew, or cared, nothing for rules.

But one Elizabethan did. When Dr. Johnson was challenged, when he planned a *Dictionary of the English Language*, for attempting single-handed in, as he hoped, three years such a work as had taken the French Academy of forty members forty years to perform, he replied that ' as three to 1600 so was the proportion of an Englishman to a Frenchman.' His namesake of the sixteenth century might have made a similar boast. What the French Academy, backed by the authority of Richelieu, had achieved in France Jonson undertook to do single-handed in England. Pressure there was none as in Corneille's case, but opportunity was, I think, offered him by the performances of the Children's companies before more select audiences. Discarding his earlier work of which we know only some names, perhaps some scenes in the *Spanish Tragedy*, and one comedy based on Plautus which he did not include in his collected ' Works ' (as he was chaffed for calling his ' Plays '), he undertook with *Everyman in his Humour* the reform of English comedy and, when the personal and satiric turn he gave to his comedies raised a storm and he was compelled to turn for a while to tragedy, there too it was his boast that his were 'legitimate poems'. It is of these alone that I will speak shortly.

To the rigour of the Unities of Place and Time Jonson did not tie himself. Unity of place was satisfied if a play which began in London or Rome remained there throughout; Unity of time meant the inclusion of the action within a limited but indefinite period. In printing the *Sejanus* and *Catiline* indeed he gave no indication of definite localities. These have been added by modern editors; but the fact is that in both Jonson's and Shakespeare's dramas one could get on quite well without any such specification of the exact room or street. The play is the thing, not the decoration. It is the other rules of classical tragedy as laid down by Castelvetro, Scaliger and Co. that he is concerned to follow, and he indicates clearly what these are: 'truth of argument', the play must be based on history not pure fiction: Jonson carries this so far that he gives chapter and verse for every scene, from Tacitus, Dio, Suetonius, Sallust, Cicero; 'dignity of persons': tragedy, the critics agreed, dealt only with persons of rank and authority, leaving to comedy ordinary persons, you and me; 'gravity and height of elocution'; and lastly 'fulness and frequency of sentence', i.e. grave moral instructions and exhortation, for so the critics seem to have understood Aristotle's *dianoia*.

The *Sejanus* and the *Catiline* do not much resemble a tragedy by Corneille or Racine. There is no such close psychological working out of a critical situation. Each is still a story play, episodic, a series of incidents leading to the death of Sejanus and his children, the failure and death of Catiline and his fellow conspirators, much as in a Shakespearian play. Jonson differs from Shakespeare mainly by the sustained dignity of the scenes—no intrusion of comic incidents like the grave-digger in *Hamlet*, or that of the porter in *Macbeth*, nor the realistic, everydaylike scenes in

Coriolanus suggestive more of London than of Rome. Nor does Shakespeare deal in political maxims and moralizing. Politics as such did not interest him, as it did Jonson. But just as in French classical tragedy one can trace the influence of the older tragi-comedy in the dominance of the love motive and the sustained element of surprise, so in Jonson's tragedies there are touches which recall the satirical comedy of the dramatist who portrayed with minute care manners and humours. Cethegus in the *Catiline* is always the head-strong, impetuous ' die-hard '. The scenes between Sempronia, Fulvia, and other women characters in the same play are quite in the manner of similar scenes in Jonson's comedies. Racine gives us no such side-lights on the character and manners of Titus or Berenice or Nero. We see them only in their relation to the main action.

Jonson's tragedies stand by themselves. They were well received except perhaps the choruses in the *Catiline*. They might, I suppose, be chanted as Miss Penelope Wheeler's young women do those in Murray's translations, though this never seemed to me quite to come off. But neither Jonson's tragedy nor his comedy left any impress of importance on Elizabethan drama. But there was another and a greater poet than Jonson who swore allegiance to the rules, always with liberties of his own. I do not mean the translator of Homer. I cannot find in Chapman's Marlowesque, bombastic tragedies any influence of theory and classical drama except it be in the lofty moral and political sentiments and the historical subject. It is otherwise with John Milton. I have cited already his confession of adherence to the critical faith as derived from Aristotle, Horace, Castelvetro; and when he came, in the *Reasons of Church Government*, to expound the various forms which a great poem, doctrinal to a nation, might take, he accepted the recognized division into Epic, Drama, and Lyric, with their chief representatives Greek and Latin. But, and here Milton stands alone, he will not allow Greek or Latin to

displace Hebrew literature even in respect of form. Along-
side Homer and Virgil he places the author of the Book of
Job as the creator of a more condensed type of epic, which
he was himself to follow in the *Paradise Regained*. Aeschy-
lus, Sophocles, and Euripides are certainly the 'three tragic
poets unequalled yet by any, and the best rule to all who
endeavour to write tragedy', but in the Bible we have
the *Song of Solomon* and the magnificent drama of the
Apocalypse. And when it comes to lyric neither Pindar nor
Callimachus is comparable to the great Hebrew Psalmists.
Still, as regards form, the classical remains dominant. Even
in his earliest published poems *Comus* and *Lycidus* Milton
follows, if not a rule yet a classical tradition, that a poet
who is meditating a great poem should try out his hand
in pastoral. So had Virgil done, so Spenser, and Pope was
later to follow their example. But it is in *Paradise Lost* and
Samson Agonistes that he is the disciple of Homer, Virgil,
and the tragedians, not excepting Seneca. I wish to consider
whether in strict truth he did well to adopt the epic of
Homer and Virgil as a model for a poem on so different
a theme and with so different a 'machinery' in the old
critical sense of that word.

But before venturing on some criticism of *Paradise Lost* I
would say a word on *Samson Agonistes*, for in it he was, I
think, nearly or entirely successful. If not the greatest, it
is with *Lycidas* the most perfect of Milton's poems, and will
bear comparison with both Greek and French tragedy, if
one grasps correctly the peculiar character of its action.
Dr. Johnson complained that, while the poem has a beginning and an end which Aristotle himself could not complain
of, it must be allowed to want a middle, since nothing passes
between the first act and the last that either hastens or delays
the death of Samson. Well, it certainly has not a middle,
an action like that of, say, the *Bérénice* or the *Britannicus* of
Racine in which you follow from speech to speech the
interplay of motives leading to the catastrophe. For

Milton's tragedy does not deal with an action of the same kind. Milton accepted, partly for personal reasons, the Church's, ultimately St. Augustine's, finding that the suicide of Samson, as they reckoned it, was justifiable only because it was directly inspired, inwardly commanded by God. What he has therefore to suggest is the gradual awakening of Samson's mind to the conviction that he has still something to do for his people and for God. We see him passing from the condition of utter despondence in which the play opens, a consciousness of his own folly and sin, his fatal weakness:

> to be weak is miserable
> Doing or suffering.

His plight is not unlike that of Ajax in Sophocles' play when he awakens to the realization of what in his madness he has done. But Samson has not lost faith in God, and when his father reproaches him with the honour he has done, or is to do, to Dagon his reply is that now the matter is in God's hand and He will vindicate Himself:

> Dagon must stoop, and shall ere long receive
> Such a discomfort as shall quite despoil him
> Of all those boasted trophies won on me,
> And with confusion blank his worshippers,

words which his father accepts as prophetic. In each of the incidents which follow, the encounter with his wife, the challenge to the boastful Harapha, we see him growing more and more his old self till the summons to appear before the Philistine lords arrives. He refuses, and then suddenly it is borne in on him that he is being guided to some great end:

> Be of good courage, I begin to feel
> Some rousing motions in me which dispose
> To something extraordinary my thoughts.

It is difficult to convey such an action in such a way as to

20

interest a normal audience. But, if one recognize it as the poet's intention, then Milton's drama is not only Greek in spirit and construction but it has something of the French movement along one line to the catastrophe.

But to return to *Paradise Lost*; when Milton finally chose the theme of the Fall, and the epic as the better form, for he had planned a drama on the subject, he accepted the critical theory of the epic—an historical subject, great persons, lofty sentiments, a lesson to the English people who, he believed, had passed through the fire to perish in the smoke. Virgil should be his model and, as that poet had done and Horace recommended, he would plunge *in medias res* and resume the earlier happenings later by way of narrative. Was it altogether a wise choice to adopt a form taken from without, at the dictation of critical theory and classical models, or might Milton have, as I have argued that Shakespeare did, let the form in which the story was to be told be determined by the character of the story itself? Certainly the classical epic form involved the poet in some serious difficulties. The central theme of the great classical epics, the *Iliad* and the *Aeneid*, is war, but the war is over when *Paradise Lost* opens and when later it is described the knowledge of that fact, and the circumstances which make any doubt as to the issue impossible, render the whole a somewhat laboured unreality relieved only by the splendid description of the Son of God going forth to battle. Again, in imitating the Ancients Milton, like Tasso, has attempted to do what Dante and the Dutch poet Vondel shrank, I think wisely, from doing, namely including the Deity among the dramatic characters, with the result that the absolute authority of God, which for the religious mind is identified with His absolute goodness, is given the appearance of a shocking arbitrariness alike in His dealings with the Angels of Heaven and poor mortals in Eden. It needs a constant effort, too, to recognize in the two mortals, who have already some of the foibles of humanity, the representatives of the whole race, to be held responsible for ' all our woe '. A great *tour de force* not only, as Keats thought in its diction, but in its whole form, I cannot believe that *Paradise Lost* will ever be again felt to have the intrinsic moral and religious value of, one is tempted to say, the *Aeneid*. It was probably impossible to make more than Milton has in the last books done of the naïve primitive story of the man, the woman, and the serpent. But one can imagine, if it would have needed a poet with the genius of Milton and a different temper of mind and experience of life, a poem in which the combat was less external, a combat for the soul of Adam, and his sin shown, less as disobedience to a sheer unreasoned command, more as the betrayal of a great trust, Adam as a forerunner, if not of Judas, yet perhaps of Peter in the hour of his weakness.

Milton was the last great poet, epic, and dramatic, whose work was influenced by the neo-classical critical doctrine, for Addison's *Cato*, which Voltaire pronounced to be our only correct tragedy, hardly counts. It was not that the doctrine was discredited, far from it. It was in full esteem in the age of Rymer and Dryden (always with qualifications suggested by the latter's own experience), Addison and Pope. Pope crystallized its two main doctrines in the *Essay on Criticism*, and by it Addison at once censured English tragedy and exalted Milton's epic. But it was becoming a kind of ' musical bank ' to which one paid respect but which had no practical influence because there was no great tragic or epic poet. The interesting and vital criticism of the period has little to do with the rules, except to point out difficulties in their observance, but it is the criticism which, foreshadowed by Jonson in his *Discoveries*, rises to importance in the critical prefaces and discussions of Dryden, the criticism which attempts to appreciate and compare the poetry of Ovid, Boccaccio, Chaucer, the French and English and Ancient dramas, criticism in which Dr. Johnson was to be Dryden's chief successor.

The *Poetics* had included no study of didactic or satiric poetry, and if the Heroic Poem was the ambition of the seventeenth century that of the eighteenth was the didactic —the *Essay on Man*, the *Art of Preserving Health*, the *Pleasures of Imagination*, the *Fleece*, the *Sugar Cane*, the *Vanity of Human Wishes*, &c., &c. Only in pastoral poetry was there a last rather interesting divergence between theory and practice. For pastoral poetry the critics *had* laid down rules. They are touched on by Dryden and Walsh in the introduction to Dryden's translation of the Eclogues of Virgil, and by Pope in introducing his own pastorals. The pastoral dealt, so said the critics, with life in the Golden Age, its aim was to describe ' a life to which we have always been accustomed to associate peace, leisure and innocence, and suffer ourselves without resistance to be transported to Elysian regions where we are to meet with nothing but joy and plenty and contentment, where every gale whispers pleasure and every shade promises repose '. So Johnson in 1750. Later he was to find among the faults of *Lycidas* that the form is that of a pastoral, ' easy, vulgar and therefore disgusting '. The fact is that beginning with Steele's review of the pastorals of Ambrose Phillips and Pope, Pope's brilliant rejoinder, and Gay's *Shepherds' Week*, there was throughout the century a steady widening of the gulf between the two principles of following nature and imitating the ancients, till Crabbe finally laid the ghost of pastoral when he insisted on painting the cot—

As Truth will paint it and as bards will not.

It is not my intention, nor have I time, to trace the disintegration of this neo-classical criticism in the work of Diderot, of Lessing, of Johnson himself, and the critics of the early century. What I wish rather to consider briefly —it would require a lecture or more to itself—is whether from the disquisitions of Wordsworth, Coleridge, the letters of Lamb (whom Coleridge pronounced a sounder critic than himself), Leigh Hunt, Hazlitt, Jeffrey and the reviewers, Keats's letters and Shelley's introductions and *Defence of Poetry*, whether there emerges any body of doctrine which might take the place of the criticism which, for long so authoritative, had dislimned and disappeared; any common principles which might be used not only as a standard by which to judge, but as the older criticism had done, as a monitor and guide, fixed laws—a breach of which constitutes an aesthetic flaw.

There was no discussion in this country, as in Germany, of the relative merits of classicism and romanticism. Our so-called romantic revival was largely a return to an older tradition in our poetry for which there had been going on a long preparation from the advent of Thomson, Dyer, Gray and the Wartons. Two questions were, however, raised in close connexion with one another, Wordsworth's challenge to the poetic diction of the century, and Coleridge's and Wordsworth's discussions of the true character and operations of the Imagination, which they were much concerned to distinguish from what they called Fancy. I do not know that there is anything in this latter distinction, on which Mr. Richards has written at length, that is not fairly obvious. The difference between fancy and imagination in the sphere of poetry is the difference in the sphere of natural science between a classification which places whales among fish because they swim in the sea and the biology which, on many and deeper grounds, classes them with warm-blooded mammals. The great thing was the recognition of the imagination as the function in the creation of a work of art, a poem, and that it has laws of its own but too deep and subtle to be formulated in readily applied rules. The unity of a poem or drama is not to be measured by rules of time and place. It is a harmony of all the elements, sensuous, intellectual, imaginative, none of which would be what it is apart from the others—diction, thought, imagery, rhythm, all are interdependent. Imagination, as Coleridge and Wordsworth and Lamb defined it, is the power which ' draws all things to one, makes things animate or inanimate, beings with their attributes, subjects with their accessories take one colour and serve to one effect'. Unity of interest, says Coleridge, ' is not properly a rule but in itself the great end not only of the drama but of the epic poem, the lyric ode, of all poetry down to the candle-flame of an epigram—nay of poesy in general as the proper generic term inclusive of all the fine arts as its species'. A poem is, as Paul Valéry states, an indissoluble union of sound and sense. Under sound I would include what are sensations of the mouth as well as of the ear. That was pointed out to me by a poet and was confirmed by a soldier who had suffered from shell shock which deprived him of the power of speech. As he recovered, he told me, he could read a poem with ease, but broke down if he attempted a paragraph in the newspaper. A good poem is sweet in the mouth and pleasant to the ear. The same harmony determines the question of unity of plot, the intermingling of comic and serious scenes, of diction, and of metre. Spingarn, e.g., declares the question of the unity of Ariosto's *Orlando* is still an open one. He seems to be thinking of unity of plot. But the plot is only one element, and not always an important one, in many poems and novels. For an inferior artist is often a better deviser of plots than a greater one. Neither Chaucer nor Shakespeare cared for the invention of plot. Their attitude was, ' Give me the plot, and I will give it dramatic interest and poetic beauty.' Coleridge adjudged the *Oedipus* and *Tom Jones* to be the two most perfect plots. Well, the *Oedipus* represents one type of plot which, with some difference, was brought to perfection in the drama of Racine, and one may pass it. But does one's enjoyment of *Tom Jones* gain much from perceiving how the various threads are brought together and the difficulties cleared up in a happy ending ? I do not think so. The harmony is in the broad picture of English life seen through a certain temperament. What is the unity of *War and Peace* ? Just the unity of human life. So do people feel and act when young and full of spirit and of hope. So does experience involve them in the unforeseen intricacies and responsibilities of life. So do they in the end, if they have come through, look back 'all passion spent', on the agitated currents of their life and barely recognize themselves.

And so with diction. Wordsworth was not wrong in stating that there is no essential difference between the diction of prose and poetry, unless we confine prose to the prose of mere information, the prose of a railway guide. His error was only in implying that there is only one kind of poetic diction. The whole history of poetic diction in the century shows how many different varieties poets may find appropriate to the effects they desire to produce, archaic, sensuous, imagist, and if the whole effect is harmonious then every single one of them is right. ' I write in verse ', says Coleridge, ' because I intend to use a diction other than that of prose '. That is a very partial truth, as Coleridge himself admits in the later *Anima Poetae*. Poets writing in metre have used every kind of diction from the archaic diction of Spenser, the dignified Latinized syntax of Milton, the imagist style ('pestered with metaphor' as Dryden would say) of Shakespeare, the conversational language of the ' metaphysicals ', the richly sensuous diction of Keats, to the colloquial slang of Kipling. There is no essential difference between the language of poetry and prose because, as Wordsworth boldly stated (to the horror of Professor Saintsbury) metre is an accident of poetry dating from its close connexion in origin with music and dancing. If there is any distinct trend in imaginative literature just now it is towards the supersession of metre, a prescribed pattern of verse, towards prose or what may be called prose, for it follows no prescribed metrical scheme. Though even when we speak of metre we must remember we are speaking abstractly. The metre of a good poem is the metre of *that* poem and of no other, even if we can call the metre of two different poems by some common name. Coventry Patmore somewhere declared that a certain metre could be used only for a certain kind of poetry, of tone. Tennyson had no difficulty in showing him that it might, used in another way, produce quite a different effect. What is there really common between the verse of *Hudibras*:

> And like a lobster boiled the morn
> From black to red began to turn

and that of the *Eve of St. Mark*:

> Upon a Sabbath-day it fell;
> Twice holy was the Sabbath-bell,
> That called the folk to evening prayer;
> The city streets were clean and fair
> From wholesome drench of April rains?

But returning to what may justly be called prose because it makes not even an affectation of metre by being printed in separate lines, that distinguished American critic Edmund Wilson in a discriminating criticism of *Ulysses* writes: ' The poet is still present in *Ulysses* ', and he quotes some sentences. ' But the conventions of the romantic lyric, of aesthetic *fin-de-siècle* prose, even of the aesthetic naturalism of Flaubert, can no longer be made to accommodate the reality of experience. The diverse elements of experience are perceived in different relations and they must be differently represented. Joyce has found for this new vision a new language, but a language which, instead of diluting or doing violence to his poetic genius, enables it to assimilate more materials, to readjust itself more completely and successfully than that of perhaps any other poet to the new self-consciousness of the modern world. But in achieving this Joyce has ceased to write verse. I have suggested, in connexion with Valéry and T. S. Eliot, that verse itself as a literary medium is coming to be used for fewer and fewer and for more and more special purposes, and that it may be destined to fall into disuse. And it seems to me that Joyce's literary development is a striking corroboration of this view. His prose works have an artistic intensity, a beauty of surface and of form which makes him comparable to the great poets rather than to most of the great novelists.' To discuss all this would need another or more than another lecture. It may be that, as criticism in the sixteenth and seventeenth centuries centred round the drama, so it may be now round the novel, the greater novels that is, that criticism will mainly gather to-day.

But my theme is the critic. What is his function if he can no longer presume to instruct, to arraign the breaker of rules fixed by Aristotle and the Ancients ? If the golden rule for poet and critic is that there is no rule ? Even the simplest rules, Purity, Propriety, Correctness, are all relative, subordinate to the broader rule laid down by Aristotle in the *Rhetoric*, that a speech or any other composition is the product of three factors, the speaker, the subject, and the audience. His function is to interpret the wayward work of genius, for human nature and life are too complex for anyone to foretell in what way a genius may or may nor succeed in achieving and communicating a new and complex harmony. It is his function, if he can achieve it, to show that a harmony has been achieved, or has not, that all the beauty of the *Idylls of the King* may yet leave one with an uneasy feeling that this is not the way in which these particular stories cried out to be told. And if a harmony has been achieved it remains for him to reveal the complexity and the value of the elements of which it is composed. The perfection of the poem is in its harmony, the unity of effect; its greatness in the number and value of the elements thus harmonized. The *Ancient Mariner*

seems to me a quite perfect poem, as Lamb at once perceived when Southey could see nothing in it but a Dutch
attempt at sublimity, and even Wordsworth was doubtful. But the *Divine Comedy* is a greater poem because it
has harmonized so much more in its picture of despair in
Hell, of ever-growing hope in the Purgatory, of all the
radiance of love and joy in the Paradise. It is a difficult
task, the critic's, and the history of criticism is strown with
mistaken judgments; difficult whether he has to try to form
a just estimate of the past, to tell why such and such a poet
has been over- or underestimated in his day, or, on the
other hand, is brought face to face with something new, a
Wordsworth, a Keats, a Tennyson. Lamb laid his finger
at once on what was best in the *Lyrical Ballads*—the *Ancient
Mariner* and the *Lines composed a few miles above Tintern
Abbey*. Lockhart was in the observatory when two stars
of the first magnitude arose in the sky and he missed them
both—Keats and Tennyson. To Crabbe the *Ancient
Mariner* (which he attributed to Lamb) seemed an interesting
attempt ' to portray madness not by its effects but by an
imitation, as if a painter to give a picture of lunacy should
make his canvas crazy and fill it with wild unconnected
limbs and distortion of features—yet one or two of the
limbs are pretty '. It was not quite otherwise that a poem
such as *The Waste Land* appeared to some of us older people.

Two tendencies the critic should fight against, though
they are invincible, prejudice and dogmatism, the wish to
pontificate. The first is that to which we older readers are
disposed: our taste is formed and a new phenomenon makes
us not only uncomfortable but too often angry. The latter
is that to which the young lean, as when Mr. Eliot and
Mr. Leavis and Mr. Herbert Read undertake the re-
valuation of our literature without condescending to give
reasons for their dogmatic findings. If a poet has appealed
in the past to judges whose worth is not to be set aside it
may be less useful to tell us that you personally do not like

the poet than to discover what it was that made such appeal
and why his work has lost interest, for doing so one may
recover a juster appreciation of some temporarily neglected
poet, a Donne or a Crabbe. Mr. T. S. Eliot tells us that
none can appreciate Shelley who has outgrown adolescence,
that he turns to Shelley now only to check a reference. The
late Professor Saintsbury was not a young man when he
died. He was, like Mr. Eliot, an ardent Christian and
Anglican. He hated all Shelley's political and religious
sentiments, yet he pronounced Shelley the quintessential
poet. How is one to explain such a divergence ? The
immediate inference would seem to be that Saintsbury was
still young when over seventy; Mr. Eliot already old before
fully seventeen, which would probably not be quite a fair
inference. On the other hand youth has claims to respect.
I always declined to speak *ex cathedra* on quite modern poets
though willing to talk about them in Societies where
student and professor could meet on equal terms, for the
young know best what appeals to them. Our tastes are to
some extent formed. If a poem makes immediate and
strong appeal to a large number of young and able readers,
as did *The Waste Land*, it behoves an older critic to give it
careful thought. He may find in the end what it is that has
attracted, if to him it still appears a highly sophisticated
work of the imagination reacting to many influences. Mr.
Richards indeed seems to hope that criticism will in the
end, by the aid of psychology, become scientific, that we
shall discover something corresponding to a piece of litmus
paper which, applied to a poem, will reveal by a change of
colour whether it is a product of Fancy or Imagination. I
doubt it. Criticism will always represent the reaction of
this or that individual mind or the mind of a period, Jaco-
bean, Victorian, to a work of the imagination, and it will
be, as with the mean in the sphere of morals, ' as the wise
man would pronounce '. From that circle it is impossible
to escape. The wise man defines the mean. The man

who correctly defines the mean is wise. Good wine is what the man with a good palate prefers. The good palate is that which recognizes good wine. So with the critics. They are the satellites which move around the poet, illuminating, transfiguring, distorting. But both poet and critic draw their light from the sun of beauty and truth, and we may be glad of both. Personally I do not share the objection often expressed just now to the critic who is in part a poet himself and describes poetically his reactions to a poem. Indeed I prefer it to much that affects to be scientific, dry, and magisterial. Why object to having two good things—*Hamlet* and Goethe or Coleridge on *Hamlet*, Johnson on Dryden and Pope and Gray, Dryden on Chaucer, Lamb on Milton, Arnold on Wordsworth and Byron, Swinburne on Coleridge and Shelley ? One cannot have too much of what is good.

The Metaphysics of Donne and Milton

The Metaphysics of Donne and Milton

THE study of a poet's metaphysic, supposing him to have had an articulate metaphysic, may or may not yield results of positive interest for the student and lover of his poetry. The metaphysics are not the poetry. They may enter into his poetry if and so far as they have quickened his imagination and been woven into the concrete and musical texture of his poetry; their value as poetry has no direct relation to their logical consistency and soundness but to their power to move and delight us. But if the poet has thus transmitted his ideas it becomes necessary to study them as it is necessary to study the myths or the history by which a poet has been inspired, not for their own sake, but to appreciate more finely the poet's use of them. Every poet's appeal to his readers depends on, takes for granted, a certain common background uniting them, the intelligibility and not only the intelligibility but the appreciation of his allusions, a common knowledge of and common feeling for the mythology, the history, the scenery, the literature to which he refers. If this background is, as in the case of Lucretius or Dante, metaphysical, that metaphysic must be understood. This has been clearly recognized in the case of Dante. Indeed Signor Croce is justified in protesting that the poetry of Dante has been sometimes sacrificed to the study of his cosmology, theology, and allegory. Milton's thought has received scanty consideration even since the *De Doctrina Christiana* was unearthed. Professor Masson did something, but his interests were historical rather than metaphysical. As the great Biblical poet, the great Puritan poet, Milton continued to be thought of by readers who little realized how boldly Milton interpreted Scripture, how different his temper on one side was from that of such Puritans as Rutherford or Cromwell or Bunyan. Sir Walter Raleigh decides that 'there is no metaphysic, nothing spiritual, nothing mysterious, except in name throughout the whole poem' and he has given little consideration to Milton's articulated philosophy. Professor Saurat has made a bold attempt to show that Milton was a daring thinker whose metaphysic colours the whole texture of his poetry.

In their articulate thought Donne and Milton stand at opposite poles from one another. Mary P. Ramsay in her *Les Doctrines Mediaevales chez Donne* (Oxford 1917) undertook to show that Donne's thought was throughout medieval, that all his doctrines could be traced to the scholastic philosophy whose roots are to be found even less in Aristotle than in the Neo-Platonism of Plotinus. For the study of Donne's poetry the analysis of his thought has the interest rather of curiosity than illumination. His use of scholastic doctrines in the love poems is more playful than serious, more perverse than reverent. He employs them not for their own sake but as a means to give witty or poetic expression to his subtly passionate or perverse moods. The interest of his love poems is poetic and psychological rather than philosophical, and the same is true of the best of his religious poems. It is in the great sermons that Donne develops most fully the doctrines he has embraced and endeavours most eloquently to assay their value. Miss Ramsay's work was mainly a study of the doctrinal element in these and in his theological essays.

To his acute interest in theological questions Donne was driven by his upbringing as a Catholic, and the position in which he found himself as he approached manhood. What forced him to an independent study of theology as early as 1592 was doubtless the prudential and patriotic necessity of deciding what was to be his attitude towards the Church of his country. Was he as a Catholic to cut himself off from all advancement, or seek preferment abroad ? He

found escape from the quandary by the way of ' enlightenment', by attaining to the view that all Churches are ' virtual
beams of one sun '. But Miss Ramsay has well brought out
the tragedy of Donne's position, the source (far more so
than any acute consciousness of the divorce which was
beginning between traditional theology and the new
science—Donne often touches on this, but with a tendency
to suspect science rather than revelation) of his undecided
attitude towards the ministry. An enlightened tolerance
made it possible for him to enter the Anglican Church, and
then he discovered that this was not enough. He must
become an active champion of that Church and the apolo-
gist of persecution. It is the invariable lot of the man of
open mind. To be a good party man one must be guided
by tradition, prejudice and self-interest, keeping the open
mind for other fields. Patriotism and perhaps personal
feelings made him the sincere enemy of the Jesuits, against
whom he directed the brilliant and coarse satire of *Ignatius
his Conclave*. But the *Pseudo-Martyr* is a laboured and
unconvincing piece of task-work.

When Donne escaped from the barren field of controversy and became a great and edifying preacher he carried
with him the main body of Catholic theology. Miss Ramsay's chief work in the chapters which follow those on his
life was to show that the views, which he discusses or
defends, on the creation of the world, on our knowledge
of God, on angels, their substance and functions, on the
human soul and its connexion with the body, on ecstasy,
have behind them a long tradition of discussions and definitions scholastic and Neo-Platonic. Setting aside one or
two doctrines which represented to the Anglicans the errors
of Rome—Transubstantiation, the Papacy, Purgatory, the
Cult of the Virgin and Saints—Donne finds in the definitions
of Catholic theology the answer to endless questions raised
by the restless wit of man given by reason, ' the philosopher ',
controlled by the appeal to Scripture and the Christian

consciousness. The view, for example, on which Donne insists in poems and sermons alike, of the relation of mind and body, his refusal to depreciate the body, is not so individual as a hazy idea of medieval asceticism might suggest. It is the reasoned conclusion of St. Augustine, the greatest shaper of medieval theology. Donne's aim as a preacher is to define and illuminate by his learning and his imagination the great Catholic doctrines of God and Man, of sin and redemption, of death and the resurrection, not to cut out a path of his own; and he is happier and more eloquent when so employed than when denouncing Romish errors. The spirit in which he works, too, is neither mystical nor rationalist but the spirit of the great Catholic theologians who have always taken reason as the portal to faith, as not contradicted but transcended by revelation. The scepticism of Donne, on which modern criticism insists, was not the rationalist, dogmatic scepticism of the later deists and sceptics. It was that profounder, temperamental and spiritual, scepticism which torments the soul that realizes too vividly the contradictions besetting all human speculation, the uncertainty of human values, the inextricable interweaving of good and evil—evil begetting good, good begetting evil:

> There's nothing simply good nor ill alone:
> Of every quality comparison
> The only measure is, and judge opinion.

It was a mood, as Donne says, to be overcome, not reasoned with.

Milton had far more of the temper of the new rationalism, the dogmatism of the great individual system-builders from Descartes and Spinoza to Hegel. The Catholic tradition to which Donne always rallies is rejected by Milton without compunction. As M. Saurat says, ' On trouve dans tout le Traité de la doctrine . . . une sorte de joie féroce d'iconoclaste, presque une jubilation juvénile derrière les termes raides et compassés et les textes accumulés, dans la destruction des idées orthodoxes'. Most of the great doctrines which Donne accepts as the orthodox finding of th Christian Church—the possibility of attaining to a knowledge of God by reason, the Trinity, the creation of the world from nothing, the origin of the individual soul— Milton flatly rejects. God the Infinite is unknowable. He has 'expressed himself' in the Son, but the Son is not God, is separated from God by the gulf which parts the finite and the infinite. The world was not created from nothing but from God, of whose substance matter is, therefore, a part. Matter and spirit are not distinct. The one passes as it grows finer into the other:

> one first matter all
> Indu'd with various forms, various degrees
> Of substance, and in things that live of life:
> But more refin'd, more spiritous and pure
> As nearer to Him plac'd, or nearer tending.

At the centre of all Milton's thought lies the determination to establish the freedom of man's will as for him the sole ultimate vindication of the justice of God. That justification of God's ways to men which *Paradise Lost* was to make luminous is wholly contained in the speech in the third book where God divests himself of responsibility for the free actions of angels and men (III, 95 f.). Milton's metaphysics are the endeavour to find a secure basis for this entire freedom. Hence his theory of creation which M. Saurat has for the first time fully emphasized, the doctrine of God's 'retreat' or 'retirement'. The source of all finite, individual being is God's withdrawal of his controlling will from a portion of his own being. 'Les parties de Dieu ainsi libérées de sa volonté deviennent les êtres' (II, I, p. 134):

> Boundless the deep, because I am who fill
> Infinitude, nor vacuous the space,

Though, I uncircumscribed myself, retire
And put not forth my goodness, which is free
To act or not, Necessity and Chance
Approach me not, and what I will is Fate.   VII, 168.

It is a strange theory and the word 'retreat' as incomprehensible as 'procession of the Holy Ghost'. It even suggests that the created universe is a bad dream of God when he relaxed his complete self-control. But Milton's underlying motive is obvious. It is a desperate endeavour to reconcile finite freedom with infinite power, Fate and Freedom. God's predestination is no predetermination, according to Milton. He foresees how free beings will use their freedom and lays his plans accordingly. He does not decree their actions:

Freely they stood who stood and fell who fell.
Not free what proof could they have giv'n sincere
Of true allegiance, constant Faith or Love,
Where only what they needs must do appear'd,
Not what they would? What praise could they receive?
What pleasure I from such obedience paid?

The same requirement of freedom, reasonable choice, determines Milton's view of individual redemption. He will not accept the orthodox doctrine that after the fall man's freedom perished, his nature became so entirely corrupt that it was no longer in him to will or to do any good thing. Man must retain sufficient freedom of will to choose whether he will seek to return to God or not. Grace is given to *strengthen* not to *create* that will, otherwise man were again an automaton. For Milton, as M. Saurat insisted throughout, the Christian doctrine of man's fall and redemption is not only, perhaps not principally, an account of historic events but a description of what happens in every individual, the conflict between freedom and passion, the victory of passion (*Paradise Lost*), or of reason (*Paradise Regained*), or the recovery of lost freedom by the reassertion of reason (*Samson Agonistes*).

It is impossible to follow M. Saurat in his close and interesting analysis of the relation between Milton's thought and work and between the incidents of his life and both his metaphysics and poetry. The shock of his first marriage, he says, and the controversy on divorce were the fountain head of all the later currents of his thought and feeling. The one important question for us is, did Milton's metaphysics make him more or less of a great poet ? M. Saurat has no doubt. ' C'est sa plus grande originalité—et c'est une originalité très rare—d'avoir construit un système cohérent de philosophie et d'avoir en même temps transposé ce système dans une œuvre artistique de première ordre'. We confess that a careful study of M. Saurat's last chapters suggests to us rather that Milton failed to transpose his philosophical system—such as it is, daring and full of great truths if as a whole dogmatic and incomprehensible—into a great poem; and that a close study of Milton's metaphysics is interesting chiefly because it explains why, despite its wonderful art, its passionate lyrical strain, the noble ethical tone of the reflective and didactic passages, *Paradise Lost* has ceased to be classed as a great religious, a great spiritual poem justifying the ways of God to men. To vindicate this view at length is here impossible. It must suffice to state shortly (1) that, as M. Saurat himself admits, much of *Paradise Lost* is no rendering of Milton's specific ideas but myth which he has accepted and retains as a poet. M. Saurat perhaps even exaggerates the degree to which Milton uses the Bible stories without believing them. The question is a very open one. At any rate, what is greatest in the poem is just his management of the myth, the great episodes and great characters, their actions and their dramatic speeches, into which little or nothing of Milton's specific doctrines enters. These find their place chiefly in the didactic portions of the poem, where ' God the Father turns a school divine', and it is the pressure of his metaphysics which turns *Paradise Lost*, as it develops, from a great epic into more and more of a didactic poem. *Paradise Regained* is purely didactic, but in *Samson Agonistes* Milton swings passionately back to the dramatic and lyric. (2) Milton's handling of the myth produced an effect quite different from that which he was aiming at metaphysically. He has *not* justified the ways of God to men but left with every thoughtful reader, including Blake and M. Saurat, a deep impression of divine aloofness, arbitrariness, injustice. M. Saurat escapes from this difficulty in an interesting and ingenious way. The counterpart to Satan, the great champion of righteousness against passion is, he declares, not God, or Messiah, but Milton himself. ' C'est Milton et non Dieu ou le Fils qui, en analysant Satan, le terrasse.' That describes well the impression which the poem leaves, Satan and Milton—two parts of Milton's own soul—these are the vital characters. But this is just to say again that Milton has not woven his teaching into the mythical texture of his poem. The argumentative portion is adventitious. It is as if Shakespeare had told the story of Othello in such a way as to enlist our sympathies for the superhuman cunning of Iago and thought to save the situation by choral odes or monologues in which he denounced Iago. There is only one way in which Milton could counter his picture of Satan's splendid courage and power of resistance, his pride touched with sympathy; and that was to show over against it the love and goodness of God. Shylock, like Satan, runs away with at any rate modern sympathies, but for a moment Shakespeare annuls that impression when Portia pleads the beauty and the power of mercy. There is only one thing stronger than strength, physical, intellectual or passionate, and that is disinterested goodness and love-illumined wisdom. But Milton, M. Saurat justly says, ' n'était pas sentimental et n'était mystique '. That is to say he was *not* a great *religious* poet.

In *Paradise Regained* and *Samson Agonistes* M. Saurat finds proof that Milton's mind emancipating itself more and more from dogma found the essence of Christianity in the moral history of every individual in whom the conflict is waged between reason and passion. Christ has become for Milton a man. The myth of the Temptation is kept for poetical purposes. Essentially the poem is a drama of the victory of reason over passion, as the greater poem had set forth mythically the surrender of rational freedom to passion. This represents, doubtless, the trend of Milton's thought, for whom the ethical aspect of religion over-shadows the doctrinal, mystical and institutional. But it is dangerous to read Milton's three great poems as though they were Kant's three Kritiks. They are poems not dogmatic treatises. It is not clear that Milton definitely rejected historical Christianity though he interprets its ethical significance in his own way. It is not quite accurate to say that of the Crucifixion Milton ' parle très peu dans le *Paradis perdu* et pas du tout dans le *Paradis reconquis* ' (p. 191). The lines which M. Saurat quotes at p. 189 contradict this:

> But first I mean
> To exercise Him in the wilderness;
> There He shall first lay down the rudiments
> Of His great warfare, ere I send Him forth
> To conquer Sin and Death, the two grand foes,
> By humiliation and strong sufferance.

The Temptation is the preparation for the Passion; but the significance of the latter is historical and theological, it is the penalty paid for Adam's sin (*P.L.* III, 203). Of the Temptation the significance is ethical and practical. In it Christ re-established man's freedom, that power to resist passion which his grace communicates to those who seek it. Christ is indeed man in his words and deeds, but he is the Son of God in a sense that other men are not:

> thou art no Son of mortal man;
> Though men esteem thee low of parentage,

Thy Father is the Eternal King who rules
All Heaven and Earth, etc.   1, 234 f.

That Milton took all this as myth, and through it adumbrated a purely ethical reading of Christianity, is at least not proven. He was after all a poet, not a metaphysician, and chose those portions and aspects of the Bible story which lent themselves to his peculiar gifts. In *Paradise Regained* he found the opportunity of portraying his ideal of heroic wisdom and self-control in an epic after the condensed style of the *Book of Job* which he had indicated in 1641 (*Reason of Church Government*) as an alternative form to the classical. One must not infer too much from what he did not do.

Nor is it quite safe to regard *Samson Agonistes* as the third chapter in a series of religious and metaphysical adumbrations of his beliefs. It is a dramatic and lyrical poem. M. Saurat wonders that there is no reference to original sin. ' Il a abandonné la théorie du péché originel.' There is no reference to it in the Bible story. It is enough that man is capable of sin, the wisest prone to err. ' Milton rénonce aussi à l'idée du rachat par le Christ.' This again is an inference from negatives. The Catholic poet Vondel in his dramatically miserable *Samson of Heilige Wraeck* (1660) finds the chief interest of the story in its forecast of a greater champion:

Who in dying shall deal a deadly blow to death.

Milton follows the Biblical story more closely and his interest is dramatic and personal, not doctrinal. It is as risky to judge of Milton's final views by the wandering cries of Samson in his suffering, or of the Chorus in their dismay, as to read the philosophy of Shakespeare in the passionate despair of Macbeth:

Life's but a walking shadow, a poor player.

In the very spirit of the greatest Greek tragedy Milton

portrays the inscrutable workings of the divine in which yet are traceable the high purposes of justice:

> All is best though we oft doubt
> What th' unsearchable dispose
> Of highest wisdom brings about,
> And ever best found in the close.
> Oft he seems to hide his face,
> But unexpectedly returns
> And to his faithful Champion hath in place
> Bore witness gloriously.

Such a view has not been found incompatible with the Christian faith.

We do not think that M. Saurat has established his contention that Milton was a great thinker and wrote a great metaphysical poem. Milton was a bold but not a subtle thinker. In rejecting traditional doctrines as irrational he did not escape involving himself in others equally irrational. As Professor Raleigh says: ' his heresies may be reduced to a single point; the ultimate basis on which he rests the universe is political not religious.' Politics are the devil; the great forcing house of mutual hatreds and injustice. Milton's whole thought was too polemical in character to attain to satisfying wisdom, but a noble spirit of justice and faith pervades his troubled and splendid poetry. But M. Saurat's carefully documented, sane and temperate study contrasts admirably with some recent German criticism determined to find in Milton a physical and mental degenerate. Milton was a great Puritan in his love for what Emerson calls the restrictive virtues and his rejection of any intermediary between God and man. He did not share the Puritan view that all human righteousness is filthy rags, that man is saved only by the unmerited grace of Christ. He was a child of the Renaissance in his confidence in reason; a great Englishman by virtue of his faith in justice.

John Donne and the 'Via Media'

John Donne and the 'Via Media'

AS Macaulay, in his essay on Ranke's *History of the Popes*, has indicated, the full tide of the Protestant movement, or revolt, was of no long duration: ' In fifty years from the day on which Luther publicly renounced communion with the Papacy, and burned the Bull of Leo before the gates of Wittenberg, Protestantism attained its highest ascendancy, an ascendancy which it soon lost, and which it has never regained.' In 1563 the Council of Trent closed, and in the following year the Pope issued the Bull *Benedictus Deus*, and Calvin died. Luther had died in 1546.

The history [continues Macaulay] of the two succeeding generations is the history of the struggle between Protestantism, possessed of the North of Europe, and Catholicism, possessed of the South, for the doubtful territory which lay between. All the weapons of carnal and spiritual warfare were employed.... At first the chances seemed to favour Protestantism; but the victory remained with the Church of Rome. On every point she was successful. If we overleap another half-century we find her victorious and dominant in France, Belgium, Bohemia, Austria, Poland and Hungary. [Nor was this due to the force of arms alone,] but to a great reflux of public opinion.

That has remained the position ever since, allowing for a large drift from both Protestantism and Roman Catholicism towards free thought and secularism. Speaking of the Catholic Irish in Glasgow, a priest said to a friend, an Inspector of Catholic among other schools: ' Yes, we lose adherents to Socialism, not at all to Protestantism.' Looking at the question from the religious point of view alone the

49

position is well described by Dr. Johnson: ' A man who is converted from Protestantism to Popery may be sincere: he parts with nothing: he is only super-adding to what he already had. But a convert from Popery to Protestantism gives up so much of what he has held as sacred as any thing that he retains; there is so much *laceration of mind* in such a conversion, that it can hardly be sincere and lasting.' That is the Johnson the deepest strain in whose constitution was religious devotion, the Johnson who said to Boswell: ' I never read of a hermit but in imagination I kiss his feet, never of a monastery but I could fall on my knees and kiss the pavement '.

But there is another passion which in some minds can do combat with pious associations—the passion for truth. Johnson himself on another occasion said, ' I could be a Catholic: I have fears enough, but am restrained by a stubborn reasonableness.' It is a rare passion, especially in whatever appeals to the feelings. What we call to-day ' wishful thinking ' is a constant and insidious tendency. Yet there are lovers of truth, and in every mind not possessed by fanatical feeling there are moments when we recognize the transcendent claims of truth.

It was among such minds that the first movements towards reformation in the Christian Church began, strengthened by the perception of gross abuses in practice, especially the prevalence of corruption. As the commission of 1537 reported to the Pope: ' Everything could be obtained for money, however hurtful it might be to the general welfare of the Church.' Among these reformers, of whom Erasmus was a shining example, were those who desired reform in doctrine as well as in practice. But when Luther took the bit in his teeth in one direction and Ignatius in another, the reforming party within the Church was divided, and the party that would yield nothing in the direction of change in doctrine gained the upper hand and, led by the Jesuits, quickly dominated the Church. Yet among Protestants, too,

there were those who drew away from the extreme Calvinism which in the Lambeth Articles nearly gained the upper
hand. From that extreme the Church of England was saved
by Queen Elizabeth, who rejected the Articles. There were
those who sought a mean way, a *via media*. On the Continent
as the combat deepened, anything like such a position
became impossible. One must be a Catholic or a heretic. It
was with such a choice before him that Casaubon came to
England in 1610, the year in which Donne published the
Pseudomartyr.

One of the first tasks which Casaubon undertook here
was the criticism of Baronius's *Annales*, and Mark Pattison's
description of the position of the two religious rivals is just
that of Macaulay: Baronius's *Annales Ecclesiastici* was an
elaborate and highly successful reply to the *Magdeburg
Centuries*, though not a work of scholarship. ' The protestant
work had undertaken to show the history of the Church as
the growth of the spirit of evil waxing through successive
ages till it was consummated in the reign of Anti-Christ.'
The work of Baronius ' exhibited the visible unity and impeccable purity of the Church founded upon Peter and
handed down inviolate, such at this day as it has always
been '. That is how the two Churches stood opposite one
another. I have heard a clergyman of to-day declare that the
Protestant view of the Roman Church was simply that in
certain respects she was in error. That was *not* the feeling of
the great reformers. They felt that the Church of Rome
was antichrist, the Mass, idolatry; and the Church of Rome
declared that Protestants and all heretics were inspired by
the Devil: ' Sometimes he has for his emissaries and scouts
abandoned men, particularly heretics, who " sitting in the
chair of Pestilence " (Psalm i, 1) scatter the deadly seeds of
bad doctrine, unsettling and precipitating headlong their
adherents, who draw no line of distinction between vice
and virtue, and are of themselves prone to evil.' (*Catechism
of the Council of Trent.*)

What then was a man to do who did not feel sure of either of these positions ? The only appeal was that which had from the first been resorted to by the reformers, to history. But the progress of the Counter-Reformation and the Jesuits was making the appeal to history what Cardinal Manning declared it to be last century, heresy. The appeal to science was also at first heresy, as Galileo found. But it is vain to fight with science, for its pragmatic proofs are open to everyone. One cannot dismiss simply as error what drives trains and cars and aeroplanes and a hundred other things. It is more difficult to secure certainty, even practical certainty, in the field of history. But it is not so difficult to point to error, to establish error, to persuade minds capable of thinking that certain propositions are at least doubtful. It was just this which drew Casaubon to England. Here was a Church which, trying to escape the extreme of Calvinism and the extreme of Tridentine Catholicism, was making its appeal to history and the Fathers. But Casaubon had been a Protestant. Donne was by descent and training a Catholic. All his ancestors were devoted Catholics, including the sister of the greatest of English Catholic martyrs, Sir Thomas More. He was carefully educated under the eyes of Catholic relatives. His was more likely to be the experience described by Dr. Johnson. How did his conversion come about, and what line did he take in his apologetic ?

When exactly Donne abandoned the Church of his upbringing is not clear. ' I had', he writes, ' my first breeding and conversation with men of suppressed and afflicted religion, accustomed to the despite of death, and hungry of an imagined martyrdom'. If his love poems, lyrics and elegies, are his earliest poems (as it is only fair to presume), his life as a young man had not been entirely edifying. There are few poems more frankly sensual, even if something must be attributed to the reaction from Petrarchan idealism, and to the influence of Ovid. Even in these poems one can detect a knowledge of theological definitions and

affirmations that was not common, and was often over-
looked by their editors: e.g. that God can only be defined
by negatives, that angels cannot directly read the hearts of
men, what kind of bodies are assumed by angels when they
appear to men, and so on. In the Satires, which are also
early, there are sympathetic references to the hunting down
of Catholics by pursuivants, and one, the third, describes
the religious problem as it appeared to an emancipated,
honest quester for the truth:

> Seeke true religion. O where? Mirreus
> Thinking her unhous'd here, and fled from us,
> Seekes her at Rome; there, because hee doth know
> That shee was there a thousand yeares agoe,
> He loves her ragges so, as wee here obey
> The statecloth where the Prince sate yesterday.
> Crantz to such brave Loves will not be inthrall'd,
> But loves her onely, who at Geneva is call'd
> Religion, plaine, simple, sullen, yong,
> Contemptuous, yet unhansome; . . .
> Graius stayes still at home here, and because
> Some Preachers (vile Ambitious bauds) and lawes
> Still new like fashions, bid him thinke that shee
> Which dwels with us, is onely perfect, hee
> Imbraceth her, whom his Godfathers will
> Tender to him, being tender,

and he goes on to describe the careless man who either rejects
all or accepts all as being much the same. But his summing
up is significant:

> but unmoved thou
> Of force must one, and forc'd but one allow;
> And the right; aske thy father which is shee,
> Let him aske his though truth and falshood bee
> Neare twins, yet truth a little elder is;
> Be busie to seeke her, beleeve me this,

Hee's not of none, nor worst, that seekes the best.
To adore, or scorne an image, or protest,
May all be bad; doubt wisely; in strange way
To stand inquiring right, is not to stray;
To sleepe, or runne wrong, is.[1]

You are to inquire, but the safest course is to follow your fathers, the appeal to history. It must have been, I think, some time before he entered the service of the Lord Keeper, Sir Thomas Egerton, that he definitely acquiesced, and a letter to his friend Goodere shows pretty clearly the line along which Donne had moved: 'You know I never fettered nor imprisoned the word Religion; not straitening it Frierly, *ad Religiones factitias* (as the Romans call well their orders of Religion), nor immuring it in a Rome or a Wittemberg or a Geneva; they are all virtuall beams of one Sun, and wheresoever they finde clay hearts, they harden them and moulder them into dust; and they entender and mollifie waxen.' It is at least a permissible deduction from such a liberal position that one should adhere to the religion of one's country. I have known Englishmen who, coming to Scotland, have thought it their duty to adhere to the Church of Scotland. It was more tempting to do so in days when to remain a Catholic was to cut oneself off from any public office.

But if one might in this way adhere to the Church of England, it was rather different when it became a question of taking orders. That meant a complete acceptance of the doctrines of the Church you adhered to; and in the early years of the seventeenth century under James I it meant taking an active part in the controversy with Rome on the one hand and on the other with the growing strength of the Puritan opposition to the constitution and the dominant spirit of the Church. Clearly Donne had no desire to take this step. It was some state-employment he hoped for

[1] *Satyre* III, ll. 43-79.

during the years when, dismissed from the service of Egerton, he was living on his relatives or those of his wife, and doing whatever came to hand, including helping others in controversy. That his wide learning made easy, without his being in every way committed to the position in question. But in 1607, or later, Thomas Morton, Dean of Gloucester, urged him to take orders, offering to transfer to him the living he held apart from the Deanery. Donne after three days' consideration refused on two grounds: (1) ' Some irregularities of my life have been so visible to some men that, though I have, I thank God, made peace with Him by penitential resolutions against them, and by the assistance of His grace banished them my affections ', yet this is known more to Himself than to others; (2) he feels that, while one may enter the ministry for a living, the promotion of God's glory must be the *first* motive, and of that he has not a complete conviction. Gosse thinks that the difficulty was that Donne was still a Catholic, had at least joined no other Church. I do not think this is possible, but that, though reconciled to the Church, he was not ready to become a priest and a preacher in that Church. Donne did not take the decisive step till 1615, when the King had made clear to the influential people who wished to promote Donne's fortune that in the Church, and only there, he would do much for him. He was ordained in January of that year. His first important appointment was that of Divinity Reader to the Benchers of Lincoln's Inn. In 1621 he was appointed Dean of St Paul's.

What I wish to do now briefly is to indicate some of the main points in the defence of the *via media* of the Church of England which was to form one strand in his learned, subtle, crabbed at times, and eloquent preaching.

In the first place, while claiming that the Anglican Church is a branch of the Catholic Church, Donne admits that she is also a Reformed Church. Nor does he think it necessary to condemn other Protestant Churches. While claiming that the Church of England has all that the Church of Rome requires for the constitution of a regular ministry, he yet maintains that it is not necessary to condemn those who, of necessity, have had to be content with less:

not to disparage, or draw in question any other of our *neighbour Churches*, who, perchance, cannot derive, as we can, their power, and their *Mission*, by the ways required, and practised in the Romane Church, nor have had from the beginning a continuance of Consecration by Bishops, and such other concurrences, as those *Canons* require, and as our *Church* hath enjoyed. They, no doubt, can justly plead for themselves, that Ecclesiasticall positive Laws admit *dispensation* in cases of necessity . . . but Almighty God preserved us from this necessity.[1]

Nevertheless, the Church of England is with other churches a branch of that Reformed Church which came out from Rome. In a long sermon on the text ' Thou art my hiding place; thou shalt preserve me from trouble; thou shalt compass me about with songs of deliverance' (Psalm xxxii, 7), he describes how the primitive Church was kept hidden by being poor, though this did not preserve her from persecution, and he then goes on, ' *Tu absconsio, Thou art my hiding place*, sayes the Primitive Church, and so may the Reformed Church say too '.[2] Always there had been in the Church many who openly or inwardly protested against the abuses which wealth and power had generated, not least in those hiding places, refuges from persecution, viz. hermitages and monasteries. In another sermon on the text: ' And as for my flock they eat that which ye have trodden with your feet and they drink that which ye have fouled with your feet' (Ezekiel xxxiv, 19), he describes this as the

---

[1] *Fifty Sermons* (1649) p. 369.

[2] *LXXX Sermons* (1640), p. 602.

condition of those who recognized and felt the errors of
the Church, yet remained loyal:

> To whom durst they communicate that doubt? They were
> under an invincible ignorance, and sometimes under an in-
> devestible scruple. They had heard that Christ commanded *to*
> *beware of the leaven of the Pharisees*, and *Sadduces*, and so of the
> *Herodians*; that is, of the doctrines of those particular sects; of
> affirming *Fate*, and *Destiny*, and *Stoicall necessity*, with the
> *Pharisees*; of denying *Spirits*, and *Resurrection* with the *Sadduces*;
> of mis-applying the prophesies concerning the *Messias*, to the
> person of *Herod*, or any earthly King; But yet, after all this, he
> commands them to observe, and performe the doctrine of the
> *Pharisees, because they sate in Moses chaire.* . . . . They therefore
> that aske now, *Where was your Church before Luther*, would then
> have asked of the *Jews* in *Babylon*, Where was your Church
> before *Esdras*; that was in *Babylon*, ours was in *Rome*.[1]

A Protestant Church, the Church of England is also the true
Catholic Church in the sense that all things necessary to
salvation are taught there.

> The true Church is that, where the word is truly preached, and
> the Sacraments duly administered . . . [that is,] Sacraments
> instituted by Christ himself, and not those supernumerary
> sacraments, those posthume, *post-nati* sacraments, that have been
> multiplyed after: and then, that which the true Church proposes,
> is, all that is truly necessary to salvation, and nothing but that,
> in that quality, as necessary. So that Problematical points, of
> which, either side may be true, & in which, neither side is
> fundamentally necessary to salvation, those marginal & inter-
> lineary notes, that are not of the body of the text, opinions
> raised out of singularity, in some one man, and then maintained
> out of partiality, and affection to that man, these problematicall
> things should not be called the Doctrine of the Church, nor lay
> obligations upon men's consciences; They should not disturb

[1] *Fifty Sermons* (1649), pp. 210, 214.

the general peace, they should not extinguish particular charity towards one another.[1]

That indicates fairly fully Donne's attitude to the Church of Rome when he is not speaking in anger. All churches are catholic which preach the doctrine of salvation through Christ without erroneous addition or subtraction, and administer the sacraments instituted by Christ. But some churches are more catholic and perfect than others, in proportion as they have preserved or have revived the doctrines taught once, and once for all, by the Apostles, and duly administer the sacraments as instituted once, and once for all, by our Lord. On that ground he is glad to be a member of the Church of England. But no church is perfect and the division of the churches is a sore evil:

> Though to all my thanksgivings to God, I ever humbly acknowledge, as one of His greatest mercies to me, that He gave me my pasture in this park, and my milk from the breast of this church [not an entirely candid statement], yet out of a fervent and, I hope, not inordinate affection even to such an unity, I do zealously wish, that the whole Catholic Church were reduced to such unity and agreement in the form and profession established in any one of these churches (though ours were principally to be wished) which have not by any additions destroyed the foundation and possibility of salvation in Christ Jesus; that then the church, discharged of disputations, and misaprehensions, and this defensive war, might contemplate Christ clearly and uniformly.[2]

But such a union lies only in Heaven. In a beautiful sermon, preached at a christening, he dwells on the marriage of Christ to his Church and goes on:

> His end was, that *he might make it to himselfe a glorious Church*,

[1] *LXXX Sermons*, pp. 60-1.
[2] *Essays in Divinity*, IV, ed. Jessopp, pp. 131-2.

not having spot or wrinkle; but that end, must be in the end of all; here it cannot be: . . . Since as yet the whole Church says, *forgive us our Trespasses*, the Church as yet is not without spots or wrinkles. The *wrinkles* are the Testimonies of our *age*; that is, our sinne derived from *Adam*; and the *spots* are the sinnes, which we contract our selves; and of these *spots*, and *wrinkles*, we cannot be delivered in this world . . . to setle such a glorious Church, without spot, or wrinkle, holy to *himselfe*, is reserved for the Triumphant time when she shall be in possession of that beauty, which Christ foresaw in her, long before when he said, *Thou art all faire my love, and there is no spot in thee*; and when we that shall be the Children of the Mariage Chamber, shall be glad and rejoice, and give glory to him, *because the Mariage of the Lambe is come, and his wife hath made her selfe ready*; that is, we that are of that Church, shall be so clothed, as that our own clothes, shall not defile us againe; as *Iob* complaines that they doe, as long as we are in this world; for, though I make me never so cleane, yet *mine own clothes defile me againe*, as it is in that place.[1]

Against the Church of Rome Donne's charge is, so far as I can follow, that she has *added* to the articles of faith and thereby burdened men's minds, and that among these additions are serious errors: 'If a man conceive any doubt of the dream of Purgatory, of the validity of Indulgence, of the latitude of a work of Supererogation, he is as deep in the fagot, and shall be as deep in Hell hereafter as if he denied the Trinity, or the Incarnation and Passion of Christ Jesus.' Rome burdens the faithful also with the Canon Law. What is Donne's bone of contention with the Puritan dissenters? It is schism. In a country which has a church that is catholic you break away because of private fancies. You break the unity of the Church though admitting its power to bring men to Christ:

If we look well we shall see that Christ provided better for his garments than for his flesh; he suffered his flesh to be torn, but

---

[1] *Fifty Sermons*, p. 37.

not his seamless garment. There may be in many cases more mischief in disobeying the uniformity of the discipline of the church than in mistaking in opinion some doctrine of the church.[1]

So far as I can follow it, that is Donne's position as regards the different churches. He does not deny the catholicity of any church which teaches true doctrine and duly administers the sacraments actually instituted by Christ. The line he took was doubtless to a considerable extent indicated by James and political considerations. Without losing touch with the Protestant Churches of the Continent James was anxious to do all he could to conciliate Catholics. Donne's first contribution to the apologetics of the time, the *Pseudo-martyr*, was an argument to persuade Catholics that they might take the oath of allegiance to the King without injury of conscience. It is a rather dry piece of work, but contains the fullest statement regarding his Catholic upbringing and slow reconciliation to the Anglican Church. When Charles succeeded to James, and Laud became the Church's pilot, Donne was a little suspect as too conciliatory to noncon-formists, and for one sermon had to submit to some questioning by Laud and the King. But into all this, and the quickening of the pace in the conflict with the Puritans,

[1] ' Sects are not bodies, they are but rotten boughes, gangrened limmes, fragmentary chips, blowne off by their owne spirit of turbulency, fallen off by the waight of their owne pride, or hewen off by the Excommunications and censures of the Church. Sects are no bodies, for there is *Nihil nostrum*, nothing in common amongst them, nothing that goes through them all; all is singular, all is *meum* and *tuum*, my spirit and thy spirit, my opinion and thy opinion, my God and thy God; no such apprehension, no such worship of God, as the whole Church hath evermore been acquainted withall, and contented with.' (*LXXX Sermons*, p. 756).

Compare Milton, who declares boldly: ' I have never known that time in England when men of truest religion were not accounted sectaries', and in the end dedicated his *De Doctrina Christiana* to all the Churches.

I am not to go. I wish just to say one word on the crucial question of the sacrament, the Mass. That was the central point in the Protestant condemnation of Roman Catholicism as idolatrous. Speaking of the choice before Elizabeth when she came to the throne (and it was somewhat of a toss-up which side she would or should choose), Maitland says: 'Many Englishmen hated " popery ", but by this time the core of the popery that they hated was no longer the Papacy but the idolatrous Mass. The choice lay between Catholicism with its Pope and the creed for which Cranmer and Ridley died.' Elizabeth showed which side she leaned to, not only by the ardour with which she kissed the Bible, but by forbidding the Bishop who was to say Mass in her presence to elevate the Host. But the Church, as shaped by the bill for the Uniformity of Religion, was not Zwinglian, if it was not Lutheran; and Andrewes and Hooker, though rejecting transubstantiation, affirmed the *real presence* of Christ in the Eucharist. In his *Responsio ad Apologiam Cardinalis Bellarmini*, Andrewes says:

Now the King laid down that Christ is really present in the Eucharist and is really to be adored, that is the reality (*rem*) of the Sacrament, but not the Sacrament, that is the earthly part as Irenaeus says, the visible as Augustine says. We also like Ambrose adore the flesh of Christ in the mysteries and yet not it but Him who is worshipped on the altar.

So, too, Ridley who kept Cranmer from Zwinglianism:

Both you and I agree herein. That in the sacrament is the very true and natural Body and Blood of Christ even that which was born of the Virgin Mary, which ascended into Heaven, which sitteth on the right hand of God the Father, which shall come from thence to judge the quick and the dead; only we differ *in modo*, in the way and manner of being: we confess all one thing to be in the Sacrament, and dissent in the manner of being there. I confess Christ's natural body to be in the sacrament by spirit and grace. You make a grosser kind of being, enclosing a natural body under the shape of bread and wine.

Donne puts it in another way:

That bread which thou seest after the consecration is not the same bread which was presented before: not that it is Transubstantiated to another Substance (which is the heretical riddle of the Roman Church and Satan's sophistry to dishonour miracles by the frequency and multiplicity of them) but that it is severed and appropriated by God in that ordinance to another use; it is bread so as a Judge is another man upon the Bench than he is at home, in his own house.

Again:

But for the manner how the Body and Blood of Christ is there, wait his leisure if he have not yet manifested that to thee: Grieve not at that, wonder not at that, press not for that; for he hath not manifested the manner of his presence in the Sacrament to the Church.

I do not know how far Laud would have accepted Donne's first statement here, but who can find proper words ? I have sometimes wondered that the Church did not deal with the mystery of the sacrament as with that of the Godhead of Christ and say as Wycliffe did: naturally bread and wine; spiritually the body and blood.

To understand at all the violent Protestant rejection of the Mass one must, I suppose, remember the difference (as in other points of Roman doctrine) between the doctrine as carefully defined and what common people were allowed, or even encouraged, to believe. A friend of mine asked a Catholic whether to believe in the genuineness of the miracles at Lourdes was necessary. No, he said, it is not *de fide*; but every good Catholic does believe in them. Some of the old Miracle Plays or Moralities show what kinds of popular superstitions were allowed and used for edifying ends.

That Donne entirely convinced himself of the validity
of the Anglican position may perhaps be doubted. In one
sonnet he has given a glimpse of feelings that must have
haunted many minds:

> Show me deare Christ, thy spouse, so bright and clear.
> What! is it She, which on the other shore
> Goes richly painted? or which rob'd and tore
> Laments and mournes in Germany and here,
> Sleepes she a thousand, then peepes up one yeare?
> Is she selfe truth and errs? now new, now outwore?
> Doth she, and did she, and shall she evermore
> On one, on seaven, or on no hill appeare?
> Dwells she with us, or like adventuring knights
> First travaile we to seeke and then make Love?
> Betray kind husband thy spouse to our sights,
> And let myne amorous soule court thy mild Dove,
> Who is most trew, and pleasing to thee, then
> When she'is embrac'd and open to most men.[1]

But his poems, some of them, touch on these questions.
The Cross is obviously a reply to the Puritan dread of that
symbol. In his *Litanie* he includes the Virgin:

> As her deeds were
> Our helpes, so are her prayers; nor can she sue
> In vaine, who hath such titles unto you,[2]

but in the *Second Anniversary* he is definitely Protestant:

> Where thou shalt see the blessed Mother-maid
> Joy in not being that, which men have said.
> Where she is exalted more for being good,
> Than for her interest of Mother-hood.[3]

[1] *Holy Sonnets*, XVIII.
[2] ll. 43-5.
[3] ll. 341-4.

But what is best in his poems and sermons is the utterance of his deeper religious feelings.

The conclusion which Donne reached, I believe, was that from which he had started in the letter to his friend Goodere from which I quoted. As things stand there is no perfect Church, none that has not erred in some respect, none that is not a true Church despite shortcomings if ' the word is truly preached, and the sacraments duly administered.' But he has come before the end of his life to believe that in the Church of England there is as near an approach to the primitive Church or more so than is to be found in any other which has added or taken away unnecessarily. In a sermon preached before Charles he puts it clearly:

The church is the spouse of Christ: Noble husbands do not easily admit defamations of their wives. Very religious Kings may have had wives, that may have retained some tincture, some impressions of errour, which they may have sucked in their infancy, from another Church, and yet would be loth, those wives should be publikely traduced to be Heretiques, or passionately proclaimed to be Idolaters for all that. A Church may lacke something of exact perfection, and yet that Church should not be said to be a supporter of Antichrist, or a limme of the beast, or a thirster after the cup of Babylon, for all that. *From extream to extream, from east to west, the Angels themselves cannot come, but by passing the middle way between;* from that extream impurity, in which Antichrist had damped the Church of God, to that intemerate purity, in which Christ had constituted his Church, the most Angelicall Reformers cannot come, but by touching, yea, and stepping upon some things, in the way. He that is come to any end, remembers when he was not at the middle way; he was not there as soon as he set out. It is the posture reserved for heaven, to sit down, at the right hand of God; Here our consolation is, that God reaches out his hand to the receiving of those who come towards him; *And nearer*

*to him, and to the institutions of his Christ, can no Church, no not of
the Reformation, be said to have come, then ours does.*[1]

The Church of England is thus a *via media* in another sense
than as between Rome and Calvin. She is in the midway
between the corruption into which the Church of Rome
had fallen and the perfect Church of Christ. That is the
most express statement I have found of Donne's convinced
Anglicanism. For, after all, the greatest things in the poems
and in the sermons are not concerned with these points in
dispute. I do not believe Donne would have laid great stress
on them had he not been compelled to take orders. The
most moving things are those that concern another conflict
in Donne's soul. He had been a sensual young man. He had
been an ambitious man, ambitious of worldly position and
power. The note of his religious verse is passionate peni-
tence, and even in that there is a peculiar note, a note of
effort, of desire to be more penitent than he naturally is:
or to feel more conscious of forgiveness. He is tormented
by the thought of death and by something stubborn in
his own heart that only the spirit of God can relax:

> Thou hast made me, And shall thy worke decay?
> Repaire me now, for now mine end doth haste,
> I runne to death, and death meets me as fast,
> And all my pleasures are like yesterday;
> I dare not move my dimme eyes any way,
> Despaire behind, and death before doth cast
> Such terrour, and my feeble flesh doth waste
> By sinne in it, which it t'wards hell doth weigh;
> Onely thou art above, and when towards thee
> By thy leave I can looke, I rise againe;
> But our old subtle foe so tempteth me,
> That not one houre my selfe I can sustaine;
> Thy Grace may wing me to prevent his art,
> And thou like Adamant draw mine iron heart.[2]

[1] *Fifty Sermons*, pp. 236-7. [Italics mine.]
[2] *Holy Sonnets*, I.

The poet *par excellence* of the Church of England in the seventeenth century is George Herbert. Of the *via media* he has no doubts:

> I joy, deare Mother when I view
> Thy perfect lineaments and hue
>   Both sweet and bright.
> Beautie in thee takes up her place,
> And dates her letters from thy face,
>   When she doth write.
> A fine aspect in fit aray,
> Neither too mean, nor yet too gay,
>   Shows who is best.
> Outlandish looks may not compare:
> For all they either painted are,
>   Or else undrest.
> She on the hills, which wantonly
> Allureth all in hope to be
>   By her preferr'd,
> Hath kiss'd so long her painted shrines,
> That ev'n her face by kissing shines,
>   For her reward.
> She in the valley is so shie
> Of dressing, that her hair doth lie
>   About her eares:
> While she avoids her neighbours pride,
> She wholly goes on th' other side,
>   And nothing wears.
> But, dearest Mother, what those miss,
> The mean, thy praise and glorie is,
>   And long may be.
> Blessed be God, whose love it was
> To double-moat thee with his grace,
>   And none but thee.[1]

[1] *The Temple*: *The British Church.*

Herbert had had his conflicts, too, not sensual but worldly. But he came through to a peace of mind which Donne never knew till the last hours.

But *via media* in itself means nothing. The question is what is our guide and norm in seeking a *via media*. There is a *via media* which God does not approve: ' I know thy works that thou art neither cold nor hot. So because thou art lukewarm and neither hot nor cold I will spew thee out of my mouth.' A Catholic friend to whom I spoke of some of the more flagrant excesses of Roman piety answered that unless you permitted these overgrowths you were apt to kill the plant. There is some truth in that. The parable of the tares suggests that in rooting out superstition one may kill faith. On the other hand, there are great risks. When after the Russian Revolution the monasteries were invaded and the graves of martyrs opened who, they had been taught, never underwent bodily decay, the rebels found them stuffed with straw. That sort of discovery may do much more harm than restraining superstitious excesses. But to come back to my point: what was the guide by which the reformers sought to find a *via media* ? It was, as I have said, history. It was the primitive Church to which they wished to get back. That was the claim of all the reformers. ' The contention alike of Luther, of Melanchthon, of Calvin is that they are restoring the purity and simplicity of the early Church.' It is a difficult position to maintain. Where does the primitive period end ? We have come to see that in the New Testament itself we have evidence of development, change. The Gospel of St. John shows an advance on the Synoptics; the later Epistles of St. Paul differ in some beliefs from the early ones. ' All truth', said St. Thomas Aquinas, ' is contained in the Bible, some of it *explicit*, some of it *implicit*'. It has been the work of the Church under Divine inspiration to develop the implicit. What Protestants call abuses Catholics regard as enrichments. Bossuet's last words to Leibniz were: ' In conclusion permit me to beg you once more to consider seriously, before God, whether, under the supposition that the Church can err and change her decrees in matters of faith, you have any adequate means of preventing her from becoming eternally variable.' Leibniz's reply was a very bold one. 'We are glad, my Lord Bishop, to belong to this Church that is always moving and eternally variable.'

Milton and Political Liberty

Milton and Political Liberty

MUCH interesting work has been done of late[1] on the question of Milton's thought on religious and political matters, as it can be studied in *Paradise Lost* and the *De Doctrina*, which lay hidden so long and was ultimately the occasion of Macaulay's flamboyant essay in the *Edinburgh Review*. Such work has been greatly helped by the admirably complete edition of Milton's works, verse and prose, collected and uncollected, issued by the Columbia University Press, pleasant to use and easy to refer to. CE. or CM. xiv, 230 (─ Columbia Edition or Columbia Milton, vol. xiv, p. 230) is sufficient for any reader with the edition at hand. To this should be added Professor William Haller's *Tracts on Liberty in the Puritan Revolution*, 1638-1647, 3 vols., by the same Press (1934), and the same writer's *The Rise of Puritanism* (1938). The other works concerned are to some extent interlinked. They are *A Study in Milton's Christian Doctrine*, by Arthur Sewell, Professor of English Literature at Auckland University, New Zealand (1939), *The Great Argument, A Study of Milton's De Doctrina as a Gloss upon Paradise Lost*, by Maurice Kelley, Princeton University Press (1941), and *Milton and the Puritan Dilemma*, 1641-1660, by Arthur Barker, Professor of English in Trinity College of the University of Toronto (1942). The last work was done under the influence of Professor A. S. P. Woodhouse, one of whose articles on the same subject, ' Puritanism and Liberty ', reprinted from the *University of Toronto Quarterly*

---

[1] (a) *The Great Argument*, by Maurice Kelley. Princeton University Press, 1941. xiv+269 pp. 33s. 6d. (b) *Milton and the Puritan Dilemma*, 1641-1660, by Arthur Barker. University of Toronto Press. 1942. xxiv +440 pp. $3.75

(1935), has reached me. Mr. C. S. Lewis's *A Preface to Paradise Lost* is to some extent an offshoot from Sewell's work.

Two main questions are at issue, Milton's Arianism and his conception of civil and religious liberty. Was he, when he wrote the great poem, the Arian he so clearly describes himself in the *De Doctrina* ? Was he in his defence of liberty, of which he boasted in the sonnet addressed to Cyriack Skinner on his blindness, in any way or measure a precursor of either the *Aufklärung* in religious thought or the political liberalism of the nineteenth century ?

Mr. Sewell's contention is that, when he composed the poem, Milton was still the Trinitarian he certainly had been in the earliest poems and tracts, though there are signs of a changing mind; that the *De Doctrina* as we have it represents a later development; and that later still his mind underwent a further change, so that he abandoned the work which he had thought of as his most precious gift to the world: ' quibus melius aut pretiosius nihil habeo '. The last position seems to me quite untenable, but of that later if space allows.

His contention that Milton was still a Trinitarian when at work on the poem starts from a careful examination of the manuscript of the *De Doctrina*. The conclusion he comes to, if I follow him aright, is that the work underwent some three revisions, and that its final form as we have it was not reached until after 1660. The first part of the manuscript as we have it was completely transcribed by Daniel Skinner, thus losing any evidence which it might have contained of changes in Milton's thought. But in the latter part, which is still in the handwriting of Milton's secretary Jeremie Picard (with corrections in several hands), there are so many altera-tions as to suggest that, if we had the first part in the same condition, we should find similar corrections; and as Sewell discovers in the later part evidences still lingering of Milton's Trinitarianism we should find the same in the transcribed part. In the *Paradise Lost* Milton, he contends, speaks of the

Son as coequal and coessential with the Father. Kelley's book is in the main a reply to Sewell's argument, a reply which Barker accepts:

The question of the period of Milton's life with which the *De Doctrina Christiana* (as it now stands) should be associated seems to me to have been settled by Kelley's recent volume (Barker, op. cit. p. 397).

I do not propose to discuss the argument in full detail, because I myself do not think that Milton's Arianism or semi-Arianism really affects the fundamental Christianity of his faith as reflected in the poem. But I must touch briefly on a few of these contentions.

To begin with, I would point out that there are certain cautions one must have in mind in deciding on the exact significance of some of the expressions which Milton uses. First, as early as 1641, in his tracts on prelacy, Milton resolved that the Scriptures and the Scriptures only were to be for him the final test of truth, a position from which he never departed except in so far as he also accepts the guidance of the Spirit:

Under the Gospel we possess, as it were, a twofold Scripture: one external, which is the written word, and the other internal, which is the Holy Spirit, written in the hearts of believers, according to the promise of God, and with the intent that it should by no means be neglected (*De Doctrina*, 1, cap. xxx).

The written word, I say, of the New Testament, had been liable to frequent corruption, and in some instances has been corrupted through the number, and in some cases the bad faith of those through whom it has been handed down, the variety and discrepancy of the original manuscripts, and the additional diversity produced by subsequent transcripts and printed editions. But the Spirit which leads to truth cannot be corrupted, neither is it easy to deceive a man who is truly spiritual (ibid. p. 275).

Milton thought that the Old Testament text had been better preserved, not aware that all the extant Hebrew versions derive from one archetype, which is not accepted by scholars as free from error. Secondly, regarding the Scripture as the sole authority Milton in the poem uses the very words of Scripture without accepting the gloss which theologians have put upon it, or defining exactly the sense in which he is using it himself. He is writing a poem, not a thesis; that was to come later. The shining instance is the words: ' This day Have I begot ' (*P.L.* v. 603). Whether Dr. Saurat or I be right in the interpretation of these words it is certain that Milton has left them undefined. That he did not mean ' generated ' seems to me clear from the words of Abdiel:

> by whom
> As by his word the mighty Father made
> All things, even thee and all the spirits of Heav'n.

for Satan's claim to be self-begot is a lie and so acknowledged to be by Satan in the ninth book, if unwillingly:

> Whether such virtue spent of old now fail'd
> More angels to create, if they at least
> Are his created.

Mr. Barker has indeed pointed out that I was in error in speaking of ' *the* exaltation ', for that was to follow the incarnation, crucifixion and resurrection, but admits that in order to get his story of the rebellion under weigh Milton has invented a previous exaltation of the Son over the Angels. Just so Vondel, to get his story of the rebellion started, invents a proclamation of God's intention that the Son shall take on himself human form and so exalt humanity above the angels. Again, if Milton writes:

> in him all his father shone
> Substantially express'd,

he is echoing Hebrews i. 3: 'Who being the effulgence of his glory and the very image of his substance.' Can one be sure that the writer of the epistle is using the word in the exact sense of later Scholastic philosophy? Moreover, as Barker points out, Milton in the *De Doctrina* distinguishes 'substance' and 'essence':

God imparted to the Son as much as he pleased of the divine nature, nay of the divine substance itself, care being taken not to confound the substance with the whole essence, which would imply, that the Father had given to the Son what he retained numerically the same himself; which would be a contradiction of terms instead of a mode of generation (CE. XIV, 193, 12–18).

Using thus the very words of Scripture Milton is able to tell his story without a challenge to the orthodox of his day. He is not a Lucretius intent on proclaiming a new and bold philosophy. That he was to do to a certain extent later. In like manner, and this is my third caution, I think (I will not dogmatize on the point) that in the tracts he accepts at times what is not precisely his own final opinion but is the prevalent view, if he thinks it makes no essential difference. Thus Mr. Sewell makes much of the fact that in the late pamphlet, *A Treatise of Civil Power* (1659), Milton does not seem to have made up his mind that, as he was to declare in the *De Doctrina*, the whole Jewish Law is abolished for Christians (Barker, op. cit. p. 248; CE. VI, 40, 20-8). He is admitting that for many it is an open question. But he could hardly state his own opinion more clearly than he had done in the *Tetrachordon* as early as 1645:

For no other cause did Christ assure us that whatsoever things we bind, or slacken on earth, are so in heaven, but to signify that the Christian arbitrement of charity is supreme decider of all controversie, and supreme resolver of all Scripture. . . . And this indeed was the reason why Apostolic tradition in the ancient

Church was counted nigh equal to the writer's word, though it carried them at length awry for want of consideration that tradition was not left to be imposed as law but to be a pattern of that Christian prudence and liberty which holy men by right assum'd of old, which truth was so evident that it found entrance even into the Council of Trent when the point of tradition came to be discussed. And Marinaro, a learned Carmelite, for approaching too near the true cause that gave esteem to tradition, that is to say, the difference between the Old and the New Testament, the one punctually prescribing writt'n law, the other guiding by the inward spirit, was reprehended by Cardinal Pole as one that had spoken more worthy a German Colloquy than a general council. I . . . shall content me here to have shown briefly that the great and almost only commandment of the Gospel is to command nothing against the good of man, and much more no civil command against his civil good. If we understand not this, we are but crack'd cymbals, we do but tinkle, we know nothing, all the sweat of our toilsomeest obedience will but mock us. And what we suffer superstitiously returns no thanks (*Tetrachordon*, CE. IV, 135-7).

If Milton leaves this Christian attitude—which was that of Christ himself—ambiguous in the *Treatise of Civil Power in Ecclesiastical Causes* (1659), if he allows that it ' remains yet as undecided ', it need be no more than an admission that his own opinion is not shared by all whom he is addressing. He had possibly learned something from the experience of the divorce tracts, which he wished he had composed in Latin. With these cautions suggested I do not propose to discuss the divergent views of Sewell and Kelley regarding single passages. Milton's final creed was that of Wulfilas, the Moses of the Goths, and one need not, I suppose, accept the dogma of Tillemont that ' un seul homme entraîna dans l'enfer un nombre infini des Septentrionaux '. Milton's Arianism was just an aspect of his revolt against Scholastic philosophy, his resolve to abide by the Scripture:

As for the terms of trinity, triunity, coessentiallity, triperson-
ality and the like they [Arians and Socinians] reject them as
scholastic notions not to be found in Scripture, which by a
general Protestant maxim is plain and perspicuous abundantly
to explain its own meaning in the properest words belonging
to so high a matter and so necessary to be known; a mystery
indeed in their sophistic subtleties, but in Scripture a plain
doctrine.

The *De Doctrina* abounds in such passionate outbursts.
Milton's Arianism implied no depreciation of the Son in
his theology. He is the Word by or through whom all
things were made, by whose obedience and suffering man
was restored to the knowledge of truth and freedom of will
of which the Fall had bereft him.

Of much greater interest than this speculative point is the
history as, in different ways, sketched by Haller, Barker and
Sewell of Milton's thought regarding the questions on
which so many in that ' period of storm and stress seldom
equalled and probably never surpassed' were intent—
political liberty and Christian liberty and their interrelation.
It was strangely enough the question of divorce which set
Milton's mind in motion while, owing to its more personal
than general interest, it gave to his thought a slight declina-
tion, not unlike that given to the atoms in Lucretius's
materialism, from which was to emerge, after contact with
so many other minds, the whole world of his speculation
finally given shape in *Paradise Lost* and the *De Doctrina*. To
these the tract *Of True Religion, Heresy, Schism, Toleration,
&c.* (1673) and the two last poems were a kind of epilogue
composed when his hopes had been shattered by the Restoration, but began to re-quicken as Charles's Declaration of
Indulgence made all Protestant hearts to tremble.

The study of Milton's development begins with Haller's
The Rise of Puritanism, which covers the years 1570 to 1643.
Barker follows with a study of the prose pamphlets from

1641 to 1660. Sewell has views very much his own on what I have called the epilogue. Haller's is to my mind the most interesting and valuable work, just because he is not so entirely concerned with the controversies, the desperate efforts to discover the *absolutely* right government, the *absolutely* right relation between state and church. His chief theme is the spirit of Puritanism, and the means by which the preachers diffused an ideal of true religion and the good life. It has often been pointed out that, though the Restoration did bring back the King and apparently the unabated authority of the Crown, it was not really so. The first great battle for constitutional liberty had been won, and was not to be thrown away. It was the same with the Puritan cause. Apparently the Church of England had returned with its authority unabated, and Dissenters were harried and persecuted. But it did not last. Toleration became the law, and when the next great religious movement began with Whitefield and the Wesleys, it was Evangelical in religious feeling and Puritan in morals. Nor were the Evangelicalism and Puritanism confined to the Methodists and other Nonconformists. The same spirit was active in the Church, and however much in time Catholic and Sacramental beliefs and feelings might grow, the mass of the English people were and, so far as they are religious at all, still are Evangelical in their religion and Puritan in their morals, theoretically if not always in practice. It is only in our own day that that temper has begun to dissolve, here and on the other side of the Atlantic, because of the advance of physical science, the critical disintegration of the accepted sources and history of Christianity, and in addition, of late, the social disturbance which is the result of thirty years of war, open or disguised.

But to return to Milton. In the prelatical pamphlets Milton had taken the field in the cause of the Calvinism and Presbyterianism in which he had been brought up, the defence of the ' one right discipline ' laid down so clearly in the Bible. Toleration was no aim of the reformers of the

Church of England but the making of England into a Geneva, a Scotland, a New England—Presbyterian and totalitarian; and Milton is as sure as his tutor Young and the rest of them that ' Church government is set down in the Holy Scriptures, and that to say otherwise is untrue '. And then his hasty marriage and the question of divorce brought him face to face with a plain statement of Scripture forbidding divorce, a much plainer statement than any that could be cited to prove Presbyterianism of divine authority. It was a dilemma. Whereas hitherto nothing had seemed so plain as the word of Scripture, now it became necessary to show that ' there is scarce any one saying in the Gospel but must be read with limitations and distinctions to be rightly understood '; and therefore that the Scriptures require a ' skilled and laborious gatherer who must compare the words he finds with other precepts, with *the end of every ordinance*, and the general analogy of Evangelic doctrine '. I need not follow Milton through the angry controversy on divorce. If he could have secured a divorce on the ground of desertion there can be no doubt it would have been for the happiness of both parties, and there were as yet no children to consider, a consideration which is never included in any of Milton's arguments. But the crux for Milton was to get round the express words of Christ. The significant words in the above quotation are ' with the end of every ordinance '. It is the principle which Christ himself applied to the Law. ' The Sabbath was for man's sake.' But the only other Law which Christ thus frankly criticized was that of divorce, and so far from relaxing that, as he relaxed the law of the Sabbath, he apparently made it more binding. But for his own unfortunate error—the only error in the conduct of his life which Milton was ever to admit, and that is the kind of error, he tells us, to which the pious Christian is more readily exposed than the experienced man of the world—but for this, Milton would probably never have questioned the clear words of Christ. It is equally clear that if he had been a Catholic in a Catholic country, and a man of wealth and political importance, he would have got a decree of nullity as easily as many others. But now he must reason on the plain word of Scripture, and he has two main arguments. God could not through Moses have sanctioned what was sin. Therefore Christ is not rescinding the permission granted under the Law. He is speaking to the Jews of his day who have abused the permission. It was a hopeless impasse for one so determined to find in the Bible a complete theology and morality. But it launched Milton on a course which might have led him in the direction of such freer thinkers as Chillingworth and Hales, though ultimately it did not. For now, as Barker points out, the emphasis for Milton is 'not on reformation and divine prescript but on liberty and free reasoning' (Barker, op, cit., p. 75). Even the laws of God are not arbitrary. They have as their aim and justification the good of men. And Christ came to enlarge not to confine that liberty, to substitute for external negative laws the inward guidance and compulsion of virtue:

In every commonwealth when it decays corruption makes two main steps: first when men cease to do according to the inward and uncompelled actions of virtue, caring only to live by the outward constraint of law, and turn the simplicity of real good into the craft of seeming so by law (CE. IV, 75).

Every command given with a reason binds our obedience no otherwise than that reason holds (*Doctrine and Discipline of Divorce*, CE. III, 45–7).

No ordinance human *or from heaven* can bind against the good of man; so that to keep them strictly against that end is all one to break them. Men of most renowned virtue have sometimes by transgressing most truly kept the law; and wisest magistrates have permitted and dispensed it, whilst they look not peevishly at the letter but with a greater spirit at the good of mankind, if always not written in the characters of law yet engraven in the heart of men by a divine impression (*Tetra-chordon*, CE. IV, 137).

The position that the individual might claim that his marriage should be dissolved if the marriage did not fulfil the end for which marriage was created was just that on which many, including such opponents to Milton's first divorce pamphlet as Herbert Palmer (Barker, op. cit., p. 108), had defended taking up arms against the King. How much Milton's political pamphlets were inspired by the action of the Presbyterians in condemning his plea for divorce is clear from the opening words of the *Tenure of Kings and Magistrates* (1649):

If men within themselves would be governed by reason, and not generally give up their understanding to a double tyranny, of custom from without, and blind affections within; they would discern better what it is to favour and uphold the tyrant of a nation. But *being slaves within doors* no wonder that they strive so much to have the public state conformably governed to the inward vicious rule by which they govern themselves. For indeed none can love freedom heartily but good men; the rest love not freedom but licence which never hath more scope or more indulgence than under tyrants.

So almost naïvely does Milton rationalize his prejudices. There had been nothing of all this in the anti-episcopal pamphlets. There the appeal had been to 'divine prescription'. In the divorce pamphlets, as Barker indicates (p. 111): 'The basic principle of divine prescription is replaced by the basic principle of human good, temporal as well as spiritual'. Churchouted by the Prelates, a 'lesion on his pride which he never forgave' (Haller, op. cit., p. 295), he consigned them to a terrible fate in the next world, and is passionate in his defence of the 'one true discipline'. Now, churchouted by the Presbyterians, he deals with them almost equally savagely, and turns to Cromwell and the army. But Cromwell will

81

fail him too in the end and his rule be described as ' a short but scandalous night of usurpation '. It was the late Professor Raleigh, I think, who maintained that Milton's experience in the field of politics and administration (so far as he did take a part in the actual administration of things, he was at least the champion of the government) was a benefit to his poetry. Perhaps, seeing the kind of man he was. But one might argue that if he could, like Virgil, have sat a little apart, viewed the scene with a more philosophical, a more sympathetic, more understanding eye, he might not have left us as great a poem as *Paradise Lost* but perhaps more poems like the *Nativity Ode* and *Comus*. But such conjectures are idle.

Milton's justification of divorce when the end for which marriage was instituted is not fulfilled is on a par with his justification of the execution of Charles as a Tyrant:

He who marries intends as little to conspire his own ruin as he that swears allegiance; and as a whole people is in proportion to an ill government, so is one man to an ill marriage. If they, against any authority, covenant, or statute, may by the sovereign edict of charity save not only their lives but honest liberties from unworthy bondage, so well may he against any private covenant, which he never entered to his mischief, redeem himself from unsupportable disturbances to honest peace and just content ment (*Doctrine of Divorce*, CE. III, 374).

The justification of the execution of Charles is the good of the people. So, appealing to reason as a judge of the end and intention of any law or covenant, even a divine law or what claims to be so from its place in the Bible, Milton had begun to move on a line that might have made him, what he has been claimed to be, a precursor of later liberalism in thought and politics. But this was not to be, and that for two main reasons, if I follow Mr Barker aright, and my own reading of Milton. I cannot discuss his linking of Milton's thought with that of many of the thinkers of the day. The one reason was that he remained the orthodox Christian he believed himself to be to the end despite some divergence on a few purely speculative points on which he appealed to the Bible for his own conclusion. The other was his increasing distrust of the wisdom and rightly ordered will of the majority of mankind. The chief question which exercised his mind after the divorce and the regicide controversies was the right relation of church and state. We cannot understand the mind of those years if we think in terms of the generally accepted view of to-day, here and even more so in America, namely that of a secular state in which all varieties of religious belief and practice that do not lead to social disorder are tolerated. That was only to emerge after a long time from the conflict of diverging views. The aim of prelates like Laud and Presbyterians like Baxter was that the state was to be religious and Christian, the Church exercising authority in all moral questions, the Church 'the divinely inspired organ of spiritual life in human society' (Haller, op. cit., p. 11). It was of course the same in Catholic countries. Baxter's complaint was not of the tyranny of Laud so much as of the fact that the discipline of the minister in each parish was kept in check. In presbyterian Scotland and New England that was established for so long as human nature could endure it. It was the duty of the 'ranselmen' in a Scottish town to see that no one sat at home from the kirk on the Sabbath. In Connecticut a man was fined for not attending meeting, and set in the stocks for kissing his wife on the Sabbath. From the first, even in his presbyterian days, Milton was against any pains and penalties beyond those that were purely spiritual—instruction, admonition, reproof and finally excommunication, the door kept open for repentance. It was in his breach with the Presbyterians and their endeavour in the Westminster Assembly to establish a presbyterian kirk with all the authority of its predecessor that he became a champion of the complete separation of state and church but with no

83

toleration for prelacy, papacy or atheism. The thorough-going representative of toleration was Roger Williams of Rhode Island, the author of *The Bloudy Tenent of Persecution* (1644), which, with Milton on divorce, seemed to many the extreme examples of the evils of a free press. Williams went the whole length. He ' argued, not that the magistrate ought to exercise forbearance or tolerate differences of opinion, but that he is bound to allow complete freedom in religion. He must defend the civil rights, not merely of varieties of true Christians, but of " Jews, Turks, anti-christians, pagans ", even of papists, " upon good assurance given of civil obedience to the civil state ". Such rights include freedom in religious association and the expression of religious opinions ' (Barker, op. cit., p. 92). Milton no more than most of the other Puritan controversialists could accept such a solution of what Barker calls the Puritan dilemma, namely how to combine political liberty with the preservation of true religion. Both in the *Treatise of Civil Power in Ecclesiastical Cases* (1659) and in his widest extension of toleration, *Of True Religion, Heresy, Schism, Toleration and what best means may be used against the Growth of Popery* (1673), in which for the first time the now re-established Church of England is included, the basis of toleration for Milton is the acceptance of Scripture as the only ground of truth in religion:

True religion is the true worship and service of God, learnt and believed from the word of God only. No man or angel can know how God would be worshipped and served unless God reveal it; he hath revealed and taught it us in the Holy Scripture by inspired ministers, and in the Gospel by his own Son and his apostles, with strictest command to reject all other traditions or additions whatever. . . . Heresy therefore is a religion taken up and believed from the traditions of men, and additions to the word of God. Whence also it follows that of all known sects or pretended religions at this day in Christendom popery is the only or the greatest heresy: and he who is so forward to brand all others for heretics, the obstinate papist, the only heretic.

To all others, including Anabaptists, Arians, Arminians, and Socinians, he will extend toleration, ' at least then let them have leave to write in Latin '. The Church of England comes in, I suppose, under the head of Arminians, and also when he writes:

The papal antichristian church permits not her laity to read the Bible in their own tongue: *our Church* on the contrary hath proposed it to all men, and to this end translated it into English with profitable notes on what is met with obscure though what is most necessary to be known be still plainest.

Thus on religious grounds Milton will not go so far as Williams. As Barker says:

The purpose of the revolution was not for him primarily political; it was to destroy Antichrist. . . . So far as he followed the Levellers and Williams in translating Christian into natural privileges, Milton was radical; so far as he refused to accept the segregation of the spiritual and the natural he was restrictive. . . . As the revolution progressed, Milton's confidence diminished; but if he lost his faith in the English people and his sense of the imminence of Christ's coming, the idea of the Kingdom remained fixed in his mind (Barker, op. cit., pp. 188, 191, 195).

The last of these quotations touches the other source of Milton's reaction against what may be called liberalism. He had hoped for a Christian kingdom in which not only true religion would be preserved with toleration for all varieties of Protestant thought and faith, but also bringing with it many political or social reforms. As I have pointed out elsewhere, Milton in the *Defensio Secunda* approves apparently the dissolution of the Barebones Parliament and yet is in sympathy with many of their aims. If he pins his faith on

Cromwell: 'you alone remain', it is in the hope that Cromwell will carry out his programme: the abolition of tithes and the abrogation of many laws. As Cromwell failed him, and it became ever more clear that the majority of the English people did *not* share his approval of the execution of the king, his contempt of the majority became ever stronger:

Who denies that there may be times in which the vicious may constitute the majority of the citizens, who would rather follow Catiline or Antony than the more virtuous part of the Senate? But are not good citizens on this account to oppose the bad with vigour and decision? Ought they not to be less deterred by the smallness of their numbers than they are animated by the goodness of their cause?

(*Defensio Secunda*, CE VIII, 176).

Milton found the solution of the problem of liberty in the Christian doctrine of the Fall, which for him, as for Johnson, as for Newman, as for the late Lord Salisbury, as for the Christian revival of to-day, was the solution of the insoluble problem of evil. See Mr. C. S. Lewis on the problem of pain. But he drew from that doctrine more than, I suppose, most Christians would do to-day. True liberty is Christian liberty, and that not only for the individual but for the state. Only the regenerate have recovered right reason and freedom of will, both of which were lost by the Fall of Adam. And for that reason they alone must rule. For Milton the final form of political liberty is Christian Liberty, the rule of the saints.

True freedom in religion was the chief end to be achieved by Milton's commonwealth. This end, and the civil good of men, could only be attained in a state governed in accordance with the law which is the natural counterpart of the law revealed by the Spirit and Scripture. Such a government was to be established, not by making the depraved will of the people the sovereign authority as in Harrington's system, but through an aristocracy composed of those having the law restored in their hearts and able truly to claim the privileges of Christian liberty. Though it could not be established in its perfection until Christ's second coming, a Christian commonwealth must be progressively modelled on the pattern of His kingdom. The good must therefore assert their legitimate freedom as men and Christians, and impose on the evil the external forms which accord with true natural freedom, though the evil are incapable of exercising it and would prefer slavery under superstition and corrupt will.

So Mr. Barker sums up (op. cit., p. 303). So, allowing for differences as to what constitutes true religion and what heresy, Milton comes to the same conclusion as Plato in *The Laws*, the Inquisition in Spain, the Emperor in Bohemia, Louis XIV in expelling the Huguenots. So extremes meet. It was *not* to be the English solution. As Haller says, the ultimate outcome of the Elizabethan church policy and all that followed it was to mean

that the common bond of her people would in future be not their religion but their nationality, and that the religious loyalties of the English of the ensuing age would express not their unity as Christians but their division upon various lines as Englishmen. In the long run it meant that the swarming English of the ensuing age, as they became divided even in nationality and blood, would retain only the community of language, literature and custom (Haller, op. cit., p. 7).

It is not surprising that to Professor Whitehead Milton's championship of liberty was of a kind to be prejudicial to liberty. Milton was convinced of his own regeneration and wisdom, and so could be certain that his condemnation of Bishops, defence of regicide, support now of Parliament now of Cromwell, were all justifiable, and that the desire of the English to escape from the arbitrary rule of saints and major-generals was a proof of their hopeless degeneracy, their total unfitness for self-government; and Carlyle was of the same opinion.

Of Milton's final mood of mind as expressed in the two poems which followed *Paradise Lost* Mr. Sewell, who disparages the *De Doctrina* as a source for a final appreciation of Milton's mind, and Mr. Barker, who accepts Kelley's view that the *De Doctrina* and the poem stand to one another as a systematic, scientific statement of theology to an imaginative poem cast in a mould derived from the epic tradition of Virgil, are more or less at one. His hopes for a state ruled by the saints, the regenerate, and thus enjoying true Christian liberty, being dispelled, Milton sought refuge in the inner life, the peace that comes from perfect obedience: ' A Paradise within thee happier far '. So Mr. Barker. Mr. Sewell goes farther in suggesting Milton's disparagement of his own work:

> On the later poems, as well as the *Of True Religion*, I base my view that *De Doctrina* is not an adequate statement of Milton's religious beliefs. *Paradise Regained* is simpler in statement and more direct than *Paradise Lost*; speculation is more diffident, as though it had given way to limited assurance. In *Samson Agonistes* Milton's spirit is aware of its own troubles, and he makes his peace, as it were, with both God . . . and with himself by a self-surrender, self-acceptance which argues rest after much perplexity. In both poems he returns to Scripture; we have the feeling that after all the mind as well as the will has learned a lesson of obedience.

A *return* to Scripture is a strange statement to make about one who has so continuously, massively, and at times angrily made Scripture the basis of all the theology in the *De Doctrina*. There is to my mind little evidence of any radical change of thought in the last poems if there is a change of mood; and the old fires are rather hidden than extinct. The mutual toleration of Protestants who base their beliefs on Scripture which includes now ' The Church of England ' is in the tract *Of True Religion &c.* (1673) a call for common action against the old enemy, evoked by the Declaration of

Indulgence issued by Charles, whose statements and promises were just as true and trustworthy as those of Adolf Hitler. It was Milton's contribution to the rising tide that was some five years later to throw up Titus Oates. *Paradise Regained* is the expression of Milton's feelings in their lowest mood of despondence. It is a noble poem. In Christ, ' this perfect man whom I have call'd my son ', are embodied the finest qualities of the Puritan ideal—disregard of wealth and glory, submission to the will of God and God only. But he shares Milton's bottomless contempt for humanity:

> And what the people but a herd confus'd,
> A miscellaneous rabble, who extol
> Things vulgar, and well weigh'd scarce worth the praise,
> They praise and they admire they know not what;
>
> . . . . . .
>
> The intelligent among them and the wise
> Are few—

doubtless true, but a fact fit to evoke pity as well as contempt: ' And Jesus when he came out saw much people, and was moved with compassion towards them, because they were as sheep not having a shepherd '. In *Samson Agonistes* Milton's mood of despondency is beginning to pass. He had begun his career as a controversialist with the Calvinist belief in the will of God as written in the plain text of Scripture and not by us to be disputed. In the divorce pamphlets he had somewhat modified his view: ' There is scarce any one saying in the Gospel but must be read with limitations and distinctions.' We have the right to study and find out ' the end of every ordinance.' ' No ordinance human or from heaven can bind against the good of man.' Now he swings back to the Calvinist, the Lutheran conception of God as ' that being for whose will no cause or reason is to be assigned as a rule or standard by which it acts, but it is itself the rule of all things, . . . ' (*De Servo Arbitrio*). To seek to understand the working of God in history, to say,

as Milton had said, that ' No ordinance human or from
heaven can bind against the good of man ' is:

> As if they would confine the interminable,
> And tie him by his own prescript,
> Who made our Laws to bind us, not himself,
> And hath full right to exempt
> Whomso it pleases him by choice
> From national obstriction, without taint
> Of sin or legal debt;
> For with his own laws he can best dispense.

But God will avenge himself upon his enemies, Samson's
enemies and, he is beginning to hope, Milton's. He has not
forgotten his old enemies, Lords and Priests:

> Lords are lordliest in their wine;
> And the well-feasted priest then soonest fir'd
> With zeal, if aught Religion seem concern'd:
> No less the people on their holy-days
> Impetuous, insolent, unquenchable.

Revenge is the dominant note of Milton's last poem:

> Samson hath quit himself
> Like Samson, and heroically hath finished
> A life heroic on his enemies
> Fully reveng'd, hath left them years of mourning.

One Christian virtue Milton never learned, humility.
Through one experience of the Evangelical Christian,
whether Puritan in the seventeenth century or Wesleyan in
the eighteenth, Milton never passed:

He thought of divine inspiration in terms of heavenly light;
but he never had the profoundly-moving religious experience,
the sense of mystical rebirth and miraculous enlightenment,
at once supernatural in its origins and enrapturing in its effects,
which provided the Puritan extremists with their energetic and

fiery zeal. . . . The typical experience of the Bedford tinker was
not for him. He never in any sense regarded himself as the
' chief of sinners '. . . . He was never the helpless and passive
recipient of divine assistance; such support came to him from
the studious summoning up of ' all his reason and deliberation '
(Barker, op. cit., cap. VI, p. 81).

But did not his reason too often rationalize the voice of his
temperament ? We are told just now very emphatically
and doubtless justly that to see in our fellow-men the
children of God is the best security of our doing our duty
to them, that Christianity is or ought to be the transcendent
sanction of Humanism. The converse is true. If we come
to regard our fellow-men with abhorrence qualified by
contempt, as in Milton's last work, or by pity, as Carlyle
confessed to Espinasse, our idea of God will suffer. The
God of *Paradise Lost* is as arbitrary in his dealings with angels
and men as Milton in his relations with his wife and his
daughters.

It has been the plan of Divine Providence to ground what is
good and true in religion and morals on the basis of our good
natural feelings. What we are towards our earthly friends in the
instincts and wishes of our infancy, such we are to become at
length towards God and man in the extended field of our duties
as accountable beings. To honour our parents is the first step
towards honouring God; to love our brethren according to the
flesh, the first step to considering all men our brethren. . . .
And we know from the highest of all authority that one can only
learn to love God whom one has not seen by loving our brethren
whom we do see (Newman).

To begin with Milton had thought of his fellow-men as
highly as of himself. It was revolutionary politics which to
a great extent warped and hardened his sympathies.

Verse Translation

Verse Translation

*with special reference to translation from Latin and
a few versions from that and other languages*

'CLEAR your mind of cant' was a piece of advice,
an injunction, which Dr. Johnson was given to
repeating. But there are shades and shades in cant. It may
be found not so much in what you say as in the stress you
lay upon it, with an implication that you are rather a
superior person in asserting with emphasis so lofty a view.
In a talk some time ago on the radio upon the debts we owed
to translation exception was at once made of translation of
verse which was waved aside as impossible. In a sense, I
suppose, it is. But the statement carries a good deal with it,
for it implies that one cannot *read* a poem in another language
with appreciation. To the best classical scholar our schools
and universities can produce, the poetry of Virgil and
Horace can never be what it was to those for whom the
Greek or Latin tongue carried with it the associations of
childhood, the intimacies of a lifetime. And even with a
modern language, unless one has been as familiar from
infancy with, say, French as with one's own tongue, there
will be a difference between the reaction of a native and one
who has acquired the language within the years of full
consciousness. A tutor at Oxford used to say to me that the
best classical poems of our scholars would, to a native, if one
were revived from the dead, appear not unlike the Babu
English poetry which some years ago afforded us amuse-
ment. Yet as a fact the corpus of English poetry includes a
considerable amount of work which is fundamentally
translated verse. The French poet, Eustace Deschamps,
saluted Chaucer as ' Grant Translateur ' on the score of his

translation of the *Romance of the Rose*. Of that translation a portion has come down to us, but we know from the *Prologue* to the *Legend of Good Women* that it had included a version, not only of the more ideal treatment of the allegory of love by Guillaume de Lorris, but also of the more cynical, and very learned, conclusion by Jean de Meun:

Thou mayst it nat denye,
For in pleyn text, it needeth nat to glose,
Thou hast translated the Romaunce of the Rose
That is an heresye against my lawe.

But the *Romance of the Rose* does not complete the tale of Chaucer's translations. The two most elaborate of his tales, *Palamon and Arcite*, or *The Knight's Tale* as it became in the Canterbury collection, and the very remarkable poem *Troylus and Criseyde* are both basically translations, but made in very different fashion the one from the other. Perhaps the best description of both would be, in terms borrowed from music, 'variations on a theme from Boccaccio'. But the variations are of a very different kind one from the other. In the *Knight's Tale* an elaborate epic poem in the classical manner, with supernatural machinery and Homeric games, is converted into a straightforward, comparatively simple story much better suited to the incidents and the *personae*. In the other a more dramatic story has its dramatic character subtly heightened and elaborated, the character of Criseyde so developed that two distinguished critics, the late Professor Legouis and the Harvard Professor Root, have taken diametrically opposite views of the heroine, the former regarding her as the innocent victim of the designs of her lecherous old uncle and of her pity, the invariable romantic preliminary to love, for her lover; while Root is convinced that she understands the whole business from the beginning and is a skilled hand at the game. Into all that I need not go, because my concern is with the poetry, of which there is abundance in both the tales, and some of it is fairly close translation. The piece of closest translation is the *Prohemium Tercii Libri*, the opening stanzas, which follow closely the song in the *Filostrato* sung by Troilus after he has won the love of Criseyde:

> O blisful light, of which the bemes clere
> Adorneth al the thriddle heven faire!
> O sonnes lief, O Joves doughter deere,
> Pleasance of love, O goodly debonaire,
> In gentil hertes ay redy to repaire.
> O veray cause of heele and of gladnesse,
> Iheryed be thy myght and thi goodnesse. . . .

Chaucer's translations are, in his poems, from French or Italian, and the genius of these languages, their syntax, especially as regards word order in the sentence, are sufficiently akin to make translation no insuperable task. It was different with Latin, and it is interesting to compare his success in the poems referred to and the laboriousness with which he endeavours, in the *Boethius*, for example, to reproduce the periodic structure of Latin prose.

Spenser's chief debt in verse translation is to French and Italian, Ariosto and Tasso taking the place of Boccaccio. Some of the loveliest stanzas in *The Faerie Queene* are renderings from Tasso. Will anyone deny the genuineness of the poetry in such stanzas as the following?

> Eftsoones they heard a most melodious sound,
>   Of all that might delight a dainty ear,
> Such as attonce might not on living ground,
>   Save in this Paradise, be heard elsewhere:
> Right hard it was for wight that did it heare,
>   To read what manner music that mote bee:
> For, all that pleasing is to living eare,
>   Was there consorted in one harmonyee,
> Birds, voyces, instruments, windes, waters, all agree.

The joyous birds, shrouded in cheareful shade,
  Their notes unto the voyce attempered sweet;
Th'Angelicall soft trembling voyces made
  To th'instrument divine respondence meet:
The silver sounding instruments did meet
  With the base murmure of the water's fall:
The water's fall with difference discreet,
  Now soft, now loud, unto the wind did call:
The gentle warbling wind lowe answered to all.

The whiles some one did chaunt this lovely lay;
  Ah see, whoso faire thing doost faine to see,
In springing flowre the image of thy day;
  Ah see the Virgin Rose, how sweetly shee
Doth first peepe forth with bashful modestie
  That fayrer seemes the less yee see her may;
Lo, see soon after, how more bold and free
  Her bared bosom she doth broad display;
Lo, see soone after, how she fades and falles away.

So passeth in the passing of a day,
  Of mortal life the leafe, the bud, the flowre,
Ne more doth flourish after first decay,
  That earst was sought to deck both bed and bowre
Of many a Lady, and many a Paramoure:
  Gather therefore the Rose whil'st yet is prime,
For soone comes age, that will her pride deflowre;
  Gather the Rose of love, whil'st yet is time,
Whilst loving thou mayst loved be with equal crime.

But the tendency after the Renaissance was to turn back
from French and Italian to their remoter sources in Latin
and Greek, though of Greek there was little first-hand
knowledge. Most of the Greek classics were edited with
Latin versions on the opposite page. Even Milton's knowledge of Greek was very limited. In editing the *Poems of*

Milton some years ago I read the Latin and Greek poems with a better classical scholar than I, the late Sir George Macdonald. He was rather shocked by Milton's few essays in Greek verse. In fact, the first English poet who was a really scholarly Grecian was Thomas Gray. But Latin influence on English poetry has a continuous history. In Latin the first popular poet was undoubtedly Ovid, but there is an interesting difference in their treatment of that poet between the medieval poets, taking Chaucer as example, and those of the Renaissance. For Chaucer Ovid was a storehouse of good tales and a master of sentiment and manners. He is not to any appreciable extent a model for style. How much Ovid's *Ars Amatoria* and *Remedium Amoris* were the source of medieval romantic love-sentiment not everyone realizes, despite the work of Gaston Paris and other scholars. We are apt to fix our attention on the ideal side of courtly, romantic love, to think of Dante and Beatrice or, on a somewhat lower level, of Petrarch and Laura, or of the fidelity in adultery of Lancelot. But in fact courtly love was in great measure a pose. The courtly lover had the same end in view as Ovid's pupils:

> It is by art ships sail the sea,
>   It is by art the chariots move,
> If then unskilled in love you be,
>   Come to my school and learn to love.
> In all the process of seduction
> This handbook gives you full instruction.

The French poets translated the *Ars Amatoria*, e.g., *Le Clef d'Amors*; and in fact the *Romance of the Rose*, the first part, is nothing more than an allegorical, abstract, courtly expansion of Ovid's doctrine of seduction, which is why Jean de Meun in the second part treats the whole doctrine and practice of courtly love in a vein of satire as sardonic and savage as that of Jonathan Swift.

Of course there are differences. Courtly love includes other elements that complicate and sometimes disguise the influence of Ovid, elements due to the different social conditions, racial and religious. Fidelity and Purity do rank higher as virtues with the medieval poet than with Ovid or the Roman poets generally. It is the Christian value attached to Purity that, in the story of the Grail, exalts Galahad above both Lancelot and Gawain. (It was not a valuation with which Chaucer had much sympathy.) But, leaving the subject of love, whether Love *par amours* or Love spiritual, as not my subject, it is as a romantic story-teller that Chaucer appreciates and uses Ovid. It may be that he took from Ovid his trick of sympathetic accompaniment, of interrupting the story with exclamations of sympathy, in which Keats was to follow Chaucer in his *Isabella, or the Pot of Basil*. But Ovid's tricks of style were fortunately beyond him. Indeed it was by a comparison of Chaucer with Ovid that Dryden was to bring the influence of Ovid in English poetry to an end. Occasionally Chaucer does translate fairly closely, as in the story of Lucretia (which probably was read by Shakespeare), but generally he retells the story in his more homely, realistic and humorous fashion. Compare his story of Ceyx and Halcyone in *The Boke of the Duchesse* with Ovid's version. Ovid tells how Juno sent Iris down to rouse Sleep and bid him send a dream to Halcyone. The light radiating from Juno rouses the sleeping god:

> tardaque deus gravitate jacentes
> Vix oculos tollens, iterum iterumque relabens,
> Summaque percutiens nutanti pectora mento,
> Excussit tandem sibi se: cubitoque levatus,
> Quid veniat (cognorat enim) scitatur, at illa:
> Somne, quies rerum, placidissime Somne Deorum,
> Pax animi, quem cura fugit; qui corda diurnis
> Fessa ministeriis mulces, reparasque labori;

Somnia, quae veras aequent imitamine formas
Herculea Trachine jube, sub imagine regis
Halcyonen adeant &c.

Chaucer gives us a dramatic, humorous little scene:

> This messager com fleynge faste
> And cried: " O, ho! awak anoon! "
> Hit was for noght; there herde hym non.
> " Awak! " quod he, " who ys't lyth there? "
> And blew his horn ryght in her eere,
> And cried " Awaketh! " wonder hyë.
> This god of slep, with hys oon ÿe
> Cast up, axed, " Who clepeth ther? "
> " Hyt am I," quod this messager.
> " Juno bad thou shuldest goon "—
> And tolde hym what he shulde doon
> As I have told yow here-to-fore;
> Hyt ys no nede reherse hyt more—
> And went hys wey, whan he had sayd.

In the last three lines Chaucer evades Ovid's rhetoric in
' Somne, quies ', etc., which Shakespeare was to translate
in *Macbeth*:

> Sleep that knits up the ravelled sleave of care,
> The death of each day's life, sore labours bath,
> Balm of hurt minds, . . .

giving it poignant significance in the mouth of Macbeth
creeping with blood-stained hands from the chamber of the
murdered Duncan. But Chaucer avoids rhetoric. In the
story of Lucretia and Tarquin Ovid exclaims:

> Quid faciet? pugnet? vincetur femina pugna.
> Clamet? et in dextra qui vetat ensis erat.
> Effugiat? positis urgentur pectora palmis;
> Tunc primum externa pectora tecta mani.

Chaucer rejects the rhetorical antitheses:

> What shal she seyn? her wit is al ago.
> Right as a wolf that fint a lomb alone,
> To whom shal she complain or mak a mone?
> What! shal she fighte with an hardy knight?
> Wel wot men that a woman hath no might.
> What shal she crye, or how shal she asterte
> That hath her by the throte, with swerd at herte?

It was at the Renaissance that Ovid's poetic rhetoric found ardent imitators among English poets, and none more so than Shakespeare. The young men from the university, Marlowe, Lyly, Peele, Greene, Daniel, and those such as Shakespeare who were drawn into their company and came under their influence, were all intoxicated by the joy of beautiful words, musical rhythms, tropes and antitheses; and, like young ladies when they first begin to take an interest in their dress, and have the management of their own allowance, they a little overdid the passion for what Wordsworth calls 'bracelets and miniature-pictures and hair-devices', whatever be the fashion of the day. Of Shake-peare's *Venus and Adonis* and the *Rape of Lucrece*, one must say that they are radically bad poems though none but a man of genius could have composed them. If Ovid could have come back to life in London in the year 1595 and read these two poems, he would have felt very much as a lady of Paris might, if, in the South Sea Islands, she met a native who had studied *Vogue* or some other dress paper. *Venus and Adonis*, as we know, is put together from Ovid's story of the same, (*Metamorphoses*, X) combined with borrowings from the stories of Salmacis' wanton appeal to the coy and passionless youth, Hermaphroditus; while the boar is described in the language which Ovid uses of the Calydonian boar killed by Meleager, which echoes the Latin poem with signal fidelity —echoes it, I would say, with an intensified reverberation. The *Rape of Lucrece*, in the same way, is elaborated from the story as told in the *Fasti*, and a comparison of the two affords an interesting study of Shakespeare's youthful art. He elaborates and embroiders in the most fantastic fashion. Six lines in Ovid's poem tell us how Tarquin was received by Lucretia, how he retired at night, and how he rose to achieve his purpose:

> Quantum animi erroris inest! parat inscia rerum
>   Infelix epulas hostibus illa suis.
> Functus erat dapibus: poscunt sua tempora somnum.
>   Nox erat; et tota lumina nulla domo.
> Surgit, et auratum vagina deripit ensem;
>   Et venit in thalamos, nupta pudica, tuos.

Shakespeare expands that into forty stanzas which, you will say, surely makes a difference ? Yes; but the devices by which he does this are just those which Ovid himself uses to tell the story of Myrrha and of others in the *Metamorphoses*, and partly in this story too—exclamations, rhetorical speeches or dialogues, antitheses, conceits. The result is a bad narrative poem considered as such. None of the Elizabethans can compare with Chaucer in the art of story-telling in verse. The Elizabethans are too intent on stylistic decoration, and Shakespeare's adornments are often in very bad taste—conceited rhetoric, antithetic points not only improbable but in their setting shocking and repellent. But we do not tend to dwell on them critically, and at times Shakespeare rises far above Ovid. His thought is juster, his rhetoric sincerer, for example, to take one passage, the verses on Opportunity (*Lucrece*, cxxvi-cxlvi).

But it is not in the narrative poems alone of this period that Ovid's influence is apparent. He dominates the two greatest sequences or collections of love poems—Shakespeare's *Sonnets* and John Donne's *Songs* and *Elegies*. But that influence is shown in very diverse ways. Nothing could be more unlike the texture of Ovid's style than that of Donne: ' for the elegancy, facility and golden cadence of poesy, *caret*. Ovidius Naso was the man, and why indeed *Naso* but for the smelling out the odoriferous flowers of fancy, the jerks of invention.' Donne was capable of jerks of invention,—very jerky jerks, but not of 'elegancy, facility and golden cadence'. What drew Donne to Ovid was, in contradistinction to the wire-drawn idealism of Petrarchan poetry, Ovid's frank and daring sensuousness. He borrows from the *Amores* and from the *Ars Amatoria* in his own harsh, coarse, and passionate elegies; and sometimes Ovid's thoughts are reproduced in a very strange setting. In one of his most Petrarchan and even Platonic poems Donne exclaims:

> First we lov'd well and faithfully,
>   Yet knew not what wee lov'd nor why,
> Difference of sex no more wee knew,
>   Then our Guardian Angel's doe;
>   Coming and going, wee
> Perchance might kisse, but not between those meales;
>   Our hands ne'r toucht the seales,
> Which nature, injur'd by late law, sets free:
>   These miracles wee did; but now alas,
>   All measure, and all language, I should passe,
>   Should I tell what a miracle shee was.

The thought:

> Our hands ne'r toucht,. . .

derives from Ovid's story of Myrrha:

> Felices quibus ista licent! humana malignas
> Cura dedit leges, et quod natura remittit
> Invida jura negant.
>
> *Met.*, x 229 ff.

Shakespeare's love-poetry is very different from that of Donne. Donne lays little stress, for a lover, on personal beauty; nor does he echo the Renaissance note of the fleetingness of beauty. For Donne, as for Dante, and perhaps Petrarch, influenced partly by Plato, partly by Christian feeling, love has in it always some mysterious earnest of immortality. Shakespeare in the *Sonnets* is obsessed by the thought of the transitoriness of all things that exist. In the reiteration of this thought, as Sir Sidney Lee pointed out, Shakespeare has drawn freely on Ovid's Pythagorean discourse on the changeable changelessness, the revolution, of all things. All I would add is that his verse seems to my ear to echo, not the rough and uncouth translation of Golding but the facility and golden cadence of Ovid's Latin:

> sed ut unda impellitur unda,
> Urgeturque eadem veniens urguetque priorem,
> Tempora sic fugiunt pariter, pariterque sequunter,
> Et nova sunt semper:

> Like as the waves make towards the pebbled shore,
> So do our minutes hasten to their end;
> Each changing place with that which went before,
> In sequent toil all forward do contend.

That is surely a closer echo of the Latin than Golding's laboured

As every wave drives others forth, and that that comes behind
Both thrusteth and is thrust himself; even so the times by kind
Do fly and follow both at once and evermore renew.

But I must not follow this theme further. Sufficient to say that if, as Arnold declared, ' Elizabethan literature is steeped in fantasy, to the lips', it is equally true to say that it is steeped in Ovid to the lips. Even the young Milton knew and loved Ovid, witness his own Latin poems. ' At first sight', says Mackail, ' no two poets could seem less alike. But if one reads the *Metamorphoses* with an eye on *Paradise Lost*, the intellectual resemblance is evident, in the manner of treatment of thought and language, as well as in the general structure of their rhetoric, in the lapses of taste and obstinate puerilities ('non ignoravit vitia sua sed amavit' might be said of Milton also) which come from time to time in their maturest work'.

The end of Ovid's dominant influence on the English poets is marked by Dryden's famous comparison of Ovid with Chaucer in the *Preface to the Fables* (1699). Yet Dryden translated considerable portions of Ovid and confesses to a fondness for his poetry: 'Whether it be the partiality of an Old Man to his Youngest Child, I know not: But they' [his renderings of Ovid] 'appear to me the best of all my Endeavours in this kind. Perhaps this Poet is more easie to be Translated than some others, whom I have lately attempted: Perhaps too, he was more according to my Genius. He is certainly more palatable to the Reader, than any of the *Roman* Wits, though some of them are more lofty, some more Instructive, and others more Correct. He had Learning enough to make him equal with the best. But as his Verse came easily, he wanted the toyl of Application to amend it. He is often luxuriant both in his Fancy and Expressions, and . . . not always Natural. If Wit be pleasantry, he has it to excess; but if it be propriety, *Lucretius*, *Horace*, and, above all, *Virgil* are his Superiours.'

Dryden's own wit had needed much curbing, and his temperament drew him to poets who were both vehement and witty. He preferred Juvenal to Horace, and hints somewhere that he might have succeeded better in translation with Homer than with Virgil. But despite Dryden's *Virgil* and Pope's *Homer*, the poet whom our classical age took most to heart was Horace, the mundane, philosophic, exquisite Horace. Virgil has always been 'princeps poetarum', but he was too great an artist to influence the medievals or the poets of the Renaissance except the greatest of them, Dante and Milton.

There are, of course, two Horaces, the Horace of the

Odes and the poet of the Satires and Epistles. On the *Odes*
I shall not venture to speak. I do not think that the genius
of our language admits of the condensation which is the
characteristic of the *Odes*. Prior is perhaps the most Horatian
of our poets, but a little too Anacreontic. Does one really
admire Milton's one attempt, or Gladstone's ? My own
favourite translator is Sir Stephen de Vere, who frankly
abandoned any attempt at condensation and took Gray's
Odes as his model. The important Horace for English
poetry is the Horace of the *Epistles* and *Satires*, the Horace
who:

> with graceful negligence
> And, without method, talks us into sense,
> Will, like a friend, familiarly convey
> The truest notions in the easiest way.

Pope indicates here one of the qualities that attracted himself
and others, the poetry which is poetry and yet is also easy
conversation. Horace has defined it himself:

> Primum me illorum, dederim quibus esse poetis,
> Excerpam numero, neque enim concludere versum
> Dixeris esse satis, neque si qui scribat uti nos
> Sermoni propriora, putes hunc esse poetam.
> Ingenium cui sit, cui mens divinior atque os
> Magna sonaturum, des nominis huius honorem.

This was the idea which appealed to the age of sense and
politeness, moderation and good form, just as Ovid's
luxuriance of fancy and wit had appealed to the young
University wits of a century earlier. But the age of Pope
was not the first to admire, or endeavour to imitate, Horace.
Even among the Elizabethans there were poets who took
Horace for their model rather than Ovid, and wrote satires
and epistles. Ben Jonson loved to call himself ' Horace ';
and Donne was the most Horatian of the Elizabethan

satirists. But the attempt to imitate Horace issued in some
rather quaint productions. Donne's *Satires* are by no means
to be despised, yet they give one the feeling that Lucilius
has come after and not before Horace. The longest of
Donne's Satires, the fourth, is obviously suggested by Horace

> Ibam forte via sacra, . . .
>
> *Sat.*, I, 9.

but instead of a bore trying to get from Horace an introduction to the influential Maecenas, Donne's bore is clearly a
spy endeavouring to detect and denounce a Catholic, and
brilliant as Donne's wit is, he could not catch the easy-
flowing, though conversational, style of Horace. The time
had not yet come.

Dryden prepared the way, but our first Horace was Pope.
He set himself to imitate Horace in his later Satires. The
result is not altogether happy. ' Between Roman images ',
says Johnson, ' and English manners there will be an
irreconcilable dissimilitude, and the works will be generally
uncouth and party-coloured; neither original nor translated,
neither ancient nor modern '. In one respect indeed Pope
excels Horace, if it be an excellence. He is a wittier and
more venomous satirist. It is very amusing to compare his
rendering of the first satire of the second book with the
original. Where Horace is complimentary, sincerely so,
Pope's satire is all the more effective that it is veiled. Further
he gets in generally about three stabs for each one of
Horace's. Horace, you will remember, consults Trebatius:
' There are who think I am too fierce in my satire and carry
things beyond lawful bounds. The other half of the world
thinks all my compositions nerveless, and that verses as good
as mine may be spun a thousand a day.' So Horace, now
Pope:

> There are (I scarce can think it but am told)
> There are to whom my satire seems too bold:

> Scarce to wise Peter complaisant enough,
> And something said of Chartres much too rough.
> The lines are weak, another's pleas'd to say,
> Lord Fanny spins a thousand such a day.

Horace has mentioned no individual person. Pope gives a passing stab to wise Peter Walters and Fr. Chartres, and then impales his old foe Lord Hervey, the Sporus of the *Epistle to Dr. Arbuthnot*. Again:

> "Take a holiday," says Trebatius to Horace.
> "Not write verse at all, you mean."
> "I do."
> "The best advice after all—may I be hanged if it isn't. But I cannot sleep."

So Horace again; and now hear Pope:

> F. I'd write no more.
> P. Not write? but then I think
>   I nod in company, I wake at night,
>   Fools rush into my head, and then I write.

Even Horace's compliments are turned to satire by Pope: Horace is recommended (I need not quote the passage at length) to sing the praises of Augustus if he must write, but declares that that is a strain above him, and that any slip would mean trouble: 'If you try to stroke him awkwardly he is on guard in every direction and his heels are ready.'

In Pope every word becomes satire of Whig poets, and of a court indifferent to literature (as the English Court has been ever since Charles II).

> Or if you needs must write, write Caesar's praise,
> You'll get at least a knighthood and the bays.
> What? like Sir Richard, rumbling, rough and fierce,
> With arms and George and Brunswick crowd the verse;

Rend with tremendous sound your ears asunder
With gun, drum, trumpet, blunderbus and thunder?
Or nobly wild, with Budgell's fire and force,
Paint angels trembling round a falling horse?

F.   Then all your Muses softer art display,
Let Carolina smooth the tuneful lay,
Lull with Amelia's liquid name the Nine,
And sweetly flow through all the Royal line.

P.   Alas! few verses touch their nicer ear;
They scarce can bear their Laureate twice a year;
And justly Caesar scorns the poet's lays—
It is to history he trusts for praise.

So again Pope applies ironically Horace's praise of Augustus to George II in his imitation of the first epistle of the second book:

While you, great patron of mankind sustain
The balanced world and open all the main;
Your country, chief, in arms abroad defend;
At home with morals, arts, and laws amend;
How shall the Muse from such a monarch steal
An hour, and not defraud the public weal?

Yet Pope is not a Horace. In the first place, he has no sincerely held and interesting philosophy to direct and control his satire. Horace's *Satires* and still more the *Epistles* have held their place in the esteem of generations not merely by their art, but by their genuine wisdom and charm, thought and feeling. Horace's ' Carpe diem ' is not an Epicurean maxim in our sense of the word ' Epicurean '. It is a lesson in moderation, taking pleasure in simple things and sitting light to the things of this world which death will soon take away:

Non es avarus, abi. . . .
Ep., II, 205–16.

' You are no miser—excellent! Well, have all the other vices fled with that one ? Is your breast free of empty ambition ? Is it void of fear and anger in the face of death? Do you smile at dreams, the terrors of magic, witches, ghosts of the night, Thessalian portents ? Do you count your birthdays with gratitude ? Do you make allowance for your friends ? Do you become gentler and better as old age draws on ? What relief is it to pluck out one thorn among many ? If you do not know how to live aright make way for those who have the skill. It is time for you to quit the scene . . . lest when you have drunk more than your fair share, you be laughed at and driven away by an age to which play is more becoming.'

Pope is too sustainedly brilliant and oratorical, even when he translates Horace closely, as in the lines beginning:

> What! armed for virtue when I point the pen,
> Brand the bold front of shameless, guilty men;
> Dash the proud gamester in his gilded car;
> Bare the mean heart that lurks beneath a star;
> Can there be wanting, to defend her cause,
> Lights of the Church, or Guardians of the Laws?
> Could pensioned Boileau lash, in honest strain,
> Flatterers and bigots even in Louis' reign,
> Could laureate Dryden pimp and friar engage,
> Yet neither Charles nor James be in a rage,
> And I not strip the gilding off a knave,
> Unplaced, unpensioned, no man's heir or slave,
> I will, or perish in the generous cause.
> Hear this and tremble! you, who scape the laws:
> Yes, while I live, no rich or noble knave
> Shall walk the world, in credit, to his grave.
> To virtue only and her friends, a friend:
> The world beside may murmur or commend.
> Know, all the distant din that world can keep,
> Rolls o'er my grotto and but soothes my sleep.

There my retreat the best companions grace,
Chiefs out of war and statesmen out of place, . . .

I. I. 105–132

or his rendering of Horace's description of the good poet in the Second Epistle of the Second Book:

At qui legitimum cupiat fecisse poema, &c.

the original of Pope's:

But how severely with themselves proceed
The men who write such verse as we can read!
Their own strict judges, not a word they spare,
That wants or force, or light, or weight, or care,
Howe'er unwillingly it quits the place,
Nay, though at Court (perhaps) it may find grace;
Such they'll degrade; and sometimes in its stead
In downright charity revive the dead.

.   .   .   .   .

Or bid the new be English, ages hence,
(For use will father what's begot by sense),
Pour the full tide of eloquence along,
Serenely pure and yet divinely strong,
Rich with the treasures of each foreign tongue;
Prune the luxuriant, the uncouth refine,
But show no mercy to an empty line;
Then polish all with so much life and ease,
You think 'tis nature, and a knack to please:
But ease in writing flows from art not chance;
As those move easiest who have learned to dance.

Indeed I venture to think that the finest product of the spirit and art of Horace in our poetry is neither Prior nor Pope, but that Christian Horace as one might call him, William Cowper. He was, of course, a far better classical scholar than Pope, a product of Westminster School, strangely and regrettably not a University man. He wrote elegant verses, and the critical principles he lays down in his letters are all in the spirit of Horace's criticism: ' To touch and retouch is, though some writers boast of negligence and others would be ashamed to show their foul copies, the secret of almost all good writing especially in verse. I am never weary of it myself.' Cowper's first English poems were didactic satires, for each of which he chose a motto from Horace or Virgil, and to my ear and mind, despite the wide interval which separates Evangelical piety from Roman Epicureanism, Cowper's satires are more Horatian than Pope's. He is more of a gentleman than Pope, urbane and sympathetic despite his alarming creed. He has, like Horace, a philosophy in which he really believes and wishes to inculcate, and though it is not Horace's creed yet it has some by-products which recall Horace—a love of retirement and the country, and a certain gentle Epicureanism, a taste, if not for Falernian wine and ' the tangles of Neæra's hair ', yet for tea and the talk of lively and sympathetic ladies. Lastly, Cowper's diction and verse come much nearer to that conversational, natural, easy, polite, humorous style which is Horace's ideal in the *Sermones.*

> " I never will believe ", the colonel cries,
> " The sanguinary schemes that some devise,
> Who make the good Creator on their plan
> A being of less equity than man.
> If appetite, or what divines call lust,
> Which men comply with, even because they must,
> Be punished with perdition, who is pure?
> Then theirs, no doubt, as well as mine, is sure.
> If sentence of eternal pain belong
> To every sudden slip and transient wrong,
> Then Heaven enjoins the fallible and frail
> A hopeless task, and damns them if they fail.

My creed (whatever some creed-makers mean
By Athanasian nonsense, or Nicene),
My creed is, He is safe who does his best,
And death's a doom sufficient for the rest."
  " Right," says an ensign, " and for aught I see,
  Your faith and mine substantially agree;
  The best of every man's performance here
  Is to discharge the duties of his sphere, &c.

Even in his shorter lyrical pieces I venture to think that
Cowper has more of the essential Horace than Prior. Prior
is more airy, more Anacreontic. But Horace is not
Anacreon. His lighter odes give to a careful reader an
impression of solidity of thought and feeling as well as of a
finished art. ' Ludentis speciem dabit—' but it is not so light
and flippant as it appears. Well, Cowper manages no such
difficult metres as Horace. His style is less clear and shining,
his diction occasionally a little dulled by the dust of eighteenth-century conventions and poetic diction. But in his
best short poems Cowper gets the essential qualities—
compression, no words are wasted; suggestion, more
thought and feeling are suggested than fully elaborated.
There is no expansiveness of heart: how simply he expresses
what was in him a profoundly tragic conviction. He is
addressing Newton:

That ocean you of late surveyed,
  Those rocks I too have seen,
But I afflicted and dismayed,
  You tranquil and serene.

You from the flood-controlling steep
  Saw stretched before your view,
With conscious joy, the threatening deep,
  No longer such to you.

To me the waves, that ceaseless broke
  Upon the dangerous coast,

> Hoarsely and ominously spoke
> Of all my treasure lost.
>
> Your sea of troubles you have past,
> And found the peaceful shore;
> I tempest-tossed, and wrecked at last,
> Come home to port no more.

Think how that would have been expressed, had the mood been theirs, by one of the Romantics, e.g. Shelley, in the spirit of the closing stanzas of *Adonais*; and add to the above Cowper's *The Castaway*:

> I therefore purpose not, or dream
> Descanting on his fate,
> To give the melancholy theme
> A more enduring date;
> But misery still delights to trace
> Its 'semblance in another's case.
>
> No voice divine the storm allay'd,
> No light propitious shone;
> When, snatched from all effective aid,
> We perished each alone:
> But I beneath a rougher sea
> And whelm'd in deeper gulphs than he.

Cowper translated Homer but of that, as of Pope's version, I do not intend to say much. It has been fully dealt with by Matthew Arnold. One insuperable obstacle to the verse translation of Homer is the fact that, to my mind, we have not really succeeded in naturalizing the hexameter, as for example we naturalized the Italian *ottava rima*, so completely that to Swinburne it seemed that we had made it our own rather than an Italian measure. And how much the verse loses when the hexameter is converted into our decasyllabics.

But if Ovid was the favourite Latin poet of early centuries, and Horace of our classical eighteenth century, with the Romantic Revival and the nineteenth century Virgil resumed his pre-eminence challenged only by the Greeks. I can remember a short time when comparison with Homer brought on Virgil an unnecessary amount of critical censure, almost contempt. But the great Virgil is not the Latin Homer, the poet of battles. It is the Virgil of especially the second, fourth and sixth books, and that is the Virgil whose influence in English poetry has been so profound that it is easy to overlook it. Milton, of course, knew his Virgil, and commentators have no difficulty in pointing out borrowings. Yet Ovid was Milton's favourite Latin poet, and in *Paradise Lost* the influence of Virgil was blended with that of the Greeks—Homer and the tragedians, and also with that of the Hebrew Prophets. For Milton's spirit was *not* Virgilian. *Pietas* was not the first and last of virtues for Milton—that was liberty, independence of thought and feeling. He had no respect for traditional thought, feeling, or ritual. It was enough for him that the Catholic Christian Church had held this or that doctrine for him to challenge it. 'John Milton to all the Churches', so he heads the *De Doctrina*; and all the conclusions he there reaches are drawn from his own reading of, for him, the one and only source of Christian thought, the Bible. But Milton was a great poet and could not but appreciate Virgil's art. Where he seems to me to come closest to Virgil is just in those rare passages where a note of tenderness enters:

Others more mild, . . .

which is a reminiscence of Virgil's:

Quin ipsae stupuere domus, . . .

lines which Landor translated so beautifully at the age of nineteen.

But to my mind the most genuine disciples and lovers of Virgil were the greatest spiritual poet of the century,

Wordsworth, and the two finest artists, Keats and Tennyson. Keats had read Virgil repeatedly at school and Virgilian influence is traceable in all his work. Is not the famous line in *Isabella*:

> So the two brothers and their *murdered* man
> Rode past fair Florence

a more or less conscious echo of:

> Illa quidem, dum te fugeret per flumina praeceps,
> Immanem ante pedes hydrum *moritura* puella
> Servantem ripas alta non vidit in herba?

The epithet *moritura* is almost as anticipative as the *murdered* of Keats. Warde Fowler claimed Tennyson as the most Virgilian of our poets and so, in respect of subtle and elaborate art, he may be. *To Virgil* is one of the noblest poems he ever wrote:

> Chanter of the Pollio glorying
>   in the blissful years again to be,
> Singer of the sunless meadow
>   unlaborious earth and oarless sea,

> Thou that seest Universal
>   Nature moved by universal mind,
> Thou majestic in thy sadness
>   at the doubtful doom of human kind.

But the poet who comes closest in spirit to Virgil is not Tennyson but Wordsworth. Wordsworth, we now know, translated early much of Virgil, and towards the end of his best period as a poet he composed two poems which the unerring insight of Lamb at once recognized as both excellent and something altogether new in Wordsworth's poetry: *Laodamia* and *Dion*. 'Laodamia is a very original poem; I mean original with reference to your own manner. You have nothing like it. I should have seen it in a strange place, and greatly admired it, but not suspected its derivation.' (Lamb.) They were both the fruit of Wordsworth's re-reading of Virgil while preparing his son for the university. But the affinity of the two poets goes deeper than either translation or deliberate imitation. Virgil and Wordsworth were both poets of *pietas* in an age of revolution and Napoleonic egoism—of *pietas* as Warde Fowler defined it, ' the sense of duty to family and state and to the deities which protect them '. ' The pious man believes in a destiny transcending his own will: to exalt every passion, however innocent, above this is a rebellion; to intensify any passion so as to disturb the appropriate calm of resignation is to act irreverently against the Gods. Lesser duties must give way to the greater; love of wife must give way to love of country; and the sorrow of bereavement must not obscure the larger issues of life.'

Wordsworth's *Prelude* is a history of the development of his soul from an instinctive trust in the goodness of nature and the natural impulses of our own nature, through a period of disillusionment and intellectual conflict, to a recovery of his faith in nature chastened and deepened. The *Aeneid*, we are told, is the history of the growth of the hero in self-control and *pietas*. Wordsworth learned his reverence, his *pietas*, from intercourse with Nature, from the early experience of the beauty, the sublimity, the ethical significance, of the great processes of nature, as he looked back on these after the struggle to find in philosophy, in Godwin, a new ethical and political philosophy. But there came a time when this sense of the glory and sublimity of Nature faded and the question arose what was to take the place of these early intuitions:

> But yet I know, where'er I go
> That there hath passed away a glory from the earth.

Mr. Garrod would have it that Wordsworth failed in this ode and in the *Ode to Duty* to vindicate a life no longer

visited by these visionary gleams. I venture to think that
he was mistaken. As a poet Wordsworth mourned the loss
of these early impressions. Every poet must regret the loss
of the freshness of early impressions. But as a man and a
poet Wordsworth saw quite well that it was not the end,
that one cannot always live in the glory of what might be
called a spiritual conversion. To feel the claim of duty as a
natural and beautiful impulse is good on occasion. To look
back and see that one has done so is a help, but we cannot
live in such moments:

> Serene *will* be our days and bright
> When love is an unerring light
> And joy its own security, &c.

To Wordsworth, Mr. Garrod declares, duty is a second
best; we seek support from that power when higher and
freer powers fail. Well, duty *is* a second best compared
with the ideal state in which our duty will be our delight.
Aristotle also will tell us that. But of that ideal state we
have, if at all, only glimpses. The man who passes through
such an experience as a conversion, such for example as is
described in Masefield's poem, whatever be its exact
significance, a conversion, a spiritual awakening, will make
a great mistake if he thinks he is always to live in this
ecstasy. Such moments are like Christian's vision from the
Hill Clear, given to strengthen him for the journey.
Wordsworth's misfortune was that his poetic power did
flag, and yet he *would* try to write in the old way and on his
first inspiring themes—Nature and the Peasantry. There is
nothing gained by an exclusive interest in the lives of simple
people. We cannot undo the work of civilization and
become all of us peasants and working men. That was
Wordsworth's delusion, and that of Tolstoi also. Wordsworth should, like Virgil, have gone on to write of those
who carried into the higher tasks of life, the more complex
conditions of civilization, the same courage and piety. He

should have written his *Aeneid* or *De Rerum Natura*. *The Excursion* is too much a duller recast of the *Prelude*. But Virgil came to the help of the English poet and inspired *Laodamia* and *Dion*, poems Wordsworthian to the core and yet also Virgilian in spirit and not altogether unworthy of Virgil in style and verse:

> He spake of love, such love as Spirits feel
> In worlds whose course is equable and pure;
> No fears to beat away—no strife to heal—
> The past unsighed for and the future sure;
> Spake of heroic arts in graver mood
> Reviv'd, with finer harmony pursued;
>
> Of all that is most beauteous—imaged there
> In happier beauty; more pellucid streams,
> An ampler ether, a diviner air,
> The fields invested with purpureal gleams;
> Climes which the sun who sheds the brightest day
> Earth knows, is all unworthy to survey.

If one turns from Latin or a modern language to Greek does one find anything like the same phenomenon, not mere translation but what springs from translation or the thought of it, a variation on the theme of the original poem ? Not at any rate, I think, to the same extent, and one reason is that it is more easy to play such variations on the work of a lesser than of a great poet, on Ovid more easily than on Virgil, on Virgil than on Homer. Of course a great poet, like Milton, will make what use he chooses of another poet's work and yet retain his own independence. In style and verse, and to some extent in sentiment, Milton is indebted to Virgil, yet to me the genius of Milton seems more akin to that of Homer. The sentiment and poetry of Virgil makes more appeal to the reader than his characters and action. Milton's sentiment is too narrowly orthodox, despite his somewhat disguised heretical beliefs, his Arianism. But in all the greatest books the characters and action have in a high measure the same kind of interest as the heroes and action of the *Iliad*—Satan, Beelzebub, Moloch, Belial, and, to save the position, at least Abdiel. Milton is more a poet of character and action than a poet of sentiment.

But to return to my proper theme, there were two works of a very different kind, that readers were not content to accept in a translation that did not go beyond Latin—the New Testament and the poems of Homer. Into the history of the translation of the former from Greek I need not go here. Swinburne declared that the translators of the Authorized Version had turned canine Greek into divine English. The translation of Homer and its possible influence is a more interesting question, or one at least requiring more examination. Two translations of Homer have secured themselves a place in English literature—Chapman's and Pope's. The latter became for some two centuries a classic. To Dr. Johnson it seemed one of the greatest works of the kind ever produced: ' The train of my disquisition has now conducted me to that poetical wonder, the translation of the *Iliad*; a performance which no age or nation can pretend to equal.' To Johnson indeed Pope's version appeared at times superior to the original: ' I suppose many readers of the English *Iliad*, when they have been touched with some unexpected beauty of the lighter kind have tried to enjoy it in the original, where alas ! it was not to be found. Homer doubtless owes to his translator many Ovidian graces not exactly suitable to his character; but to have added can be no great crime if nothing be taken away. Elegance is surely to be desired if it be not gained at the expense of dignity. A hero would wish to be loved as well as to be reverenced.' For Coleridge it had become ' that astonishing product of matchless talent and ingenuity '. Did anything come out of it, any variation obviously inspired by the work of Pope ? I do not think so except what was not altogether an advantage for English poetry. To Pope's *Homer* Coleridge attributes, in the main, the diction which Wordsworth was to christen ' pseudo-poetic diction '. No; if anything came out of the increasing study of Greek in the century which is a permanent contribution to our literature it is the Pindaric Odes of Thomas Gray.

On the whole, I think one may say, the poet of original and genuine inspiration will seldom be content with what is just translation. It is the poet who, with perhaps an easy command of the technique of poetry, style and versification, feels no particular drive to express himself either as the poet-prophet such as Milton or Shelley, or the poet-artist for whom the form itself is an inspiration, as Robert Bridges confesses it was for him, who will find an outlet in verse translation. An example is the late Andrew Lang, one of the most gifted of men. It was, we know, a disappointment to him that his poem, *Helen of Troy*, aroused no great interest. Yet the reason seems to me pretty clear. In a sermon I listened to at St. Andrews after his death it was claimed that nothing had come from his pen which might not be read by woman or child—you know the kind of pulpit eulogy. But that may indicate some defect as well as a virtue. It did confirm me in the opinion I had formed of what was wanting in his *Helen of Troy*. It was an achievement, but not of a kind I myself admire, to write of one of the passionate women of poetry and leave out the passion, to make her the innocent victim of the goddess. Is that to do her justice ? One recalls the verses of Swinburne on the historians who had spent much labour and zeal in the vindication of the character of Mary Queen of Scots:

> Strange love they have given you, love disloyal,
>   Who mock with praise your name,
> To leave a head so rare and royal
>   Too low for praise or blame.
>
> You could not love nor hate, they tell us,
>   You had nor sense nor sting:

In God's name then what plague befell us
    To fight for such a thing?

Some gifts the gods will give to fetter
    Man's highest intent:
But surely you were something better
    Than innocent!

No maid that strays with steps unwary
    Through snares unseen,
But one to live and die for; Mary
    The Queen.

But if Lang was no great original poet he was an exquisite translator in verse of poetry, classical and modern, Greek, Latin and French. He, too, experimented on what I have described as variations on a theme, calling his verses of that kind ' Ghosts ' as Calverley, I think, called his of the same sort ' Echoes '. But many are genuine translations and very happy renderings they are, for example:

BION

The wail of Moschus on the mountains crying
    The Muses heard, and loved it long ago;
They heard the hollows of the hills replying,
    They heard the weeping water's overflow;
They winged the sacred strain—the song undying,
    The song that all about the world must go—
Where poets for a poet dead are sighing
    The minstrels for a minstrel friend laid low.

And dirge to dirge that answers, and the weeping
    For Adonais by the summer sea;
The plaints for Lycidas and Thyrsis (sleeping
    Far from the ' forest ground called Thessaly ');
These hold thy memory, Bion, in their keeping,
    And are but echoes of the moan for thee.

It was the same with myself, if I may close on a personal

note. Like many another young lover of poetry I wished to be a poet myself. For poetry, as a young man, a baker, said to me when I was like others lecturing to soldiers in the first World War 'is a thing that you discover you like'. I wrote accordingly a good deal of verse, but never felt quite sure that I had the central requirement, the irresistible desire to say what was in one's heart. That impression was finally intensified when, on leaving school for the University, I met a genuine poet and learned how it went with him. He did not sit down to compose a poem trusting to find what to say. He would set out for the day's work and never arrive there because on the way he was seized by something he must say, and say in verse, though there was much to be done before he had said it as he wished. He wrote because he must, not because he wished to write poetry. What corresponded to that in my mind was that a poem by another so took possession of me that I could not rest till I had made it to some extent my own by translation. I remember how on the occasion of my first visit to Holland, when I had undertaken to write a volume on the European Literature of the early seventeenth century for Professor Saintsbury, and had learned from, I think, the late Professor Oliver Elton that this was perhaps the one period in which the literature of the Low Countries had achieved a reputation, had indeed influenced German literature, a Dutch Professor to whom I brought an introduction read me the poem of Vondel on the death of his little daughter, I was so possessed by it that I spent the following day roaming round the docks turning the Dutch into English in the metre of the original.

Quite naturally, I think, I went on to attempt other poems of that period by Hooft, Vondel and Huyghens. Much later I made the acquaintance, indeed gained the friendship, of the most eminent poet of the day, the last representative of a second period of interest in the same literature, the eighties and nineties of last century. That was the late

P. C. Boutens. I heard with great regret of his death in 1947.
One poem of his appealed to me with the same suddenness
and completeness, *Love's Hour*, a description of the periods
of a single day seen through the eyes of a pair of lovers, at
least so I interpreted the poem. As I have said I came to know
him intimately and I got into the habit of getting him to
read a poem with me and make quite clear the meaning of
every line and phrase, and then I set myself to render it to
the best of my ability, some of them rather elaborate poems
as *The Morning Nightingale*, and later another even more
elaborate poem: *The Christ-Child*.[1] Through Boutens I was
introduced to the work of more recent poets especially Dr.
Jan Hendrik Leopold and attempted two poems of a very
different kind from those of Boutens: OINOU ENA
STALAGMON: and another which was recently printed
in the periodical called *Translation*: *Cheops*. In all my
attempts of the kind, and I fancy this is the experience of
others, two things seemed to me true: it needs happy
moments for this task, &c., that is one, the other is Aristotle's
saying that Art and Chance are closely akin. A mere
printer's mistake improved a poem by Malherbe when the
line, ' Rosette a vécu ce que vivent les roses' became 'Rose,
elle a vécu, &c.' By a somewhat similar chance I once, for
a casual collection of poems and articles, attempted a sonnet
The Flute by the French Parnassian poet Heredia which has
had the fortune first to please myself and so far to please
others that, with and without application to me, it has been
reprinted more than once here and on the other side of the
Atlantic. I have come to one or two conclusions. One is,
as I have said, that there is always in success an element of
chance if also of laborious work. The other is that one
should be content with this or that poem which has taken
possession of one for the time. A complete translation of
the works of this or that poet is a tremendous and perilous

[1] These and some other translations I hope to issue privately with the
Samson Press, Woodstock, Oxford.

risk. I might add a third. A somewhat elaborate poem is more easy to translate, with at least the appearance of success, than one whose charm is its simplicity. Transferred to another tongue simplicity is too apt to become banality. Who has really achieved success with Heine ? It was, I think, a happy thought of Sir Alexander Gray to choose the Scottish dialect (it might have been another dialect, Barnes's, for example) because dialect carries with it an immediate suggestion of simplicity, the rural minstrel, the kind of poetry which wanders through local papers but which Burns suddenly exalted by the inspiration of genius and a passionate temperament. With an elaborate poem one may, sometimes with success, take liberties, find another image than the poet's which in your tongue conveys the impression of the original, may even intensify the original effect. If translation is, as has been affirmed, impossible, it is equally certain that it is impossible not at times to be tempted to defy the statement and try. One cannot, after all, rule out translation remembering what English poetry owes to the attempt, from Chaucer's *Troylus* to Fitzgerald's *Omar Khayyam*.

Index